IN BRITAIN

21ST CENTURY EDITION

MICHAEL VAUGHAN-REES

GERALDINE SWEENEY

PICOT CASSIDY

In Britain

Editor Christina Klein, Carol Goodwright
Design Wendi Watson
Cover Gregor Arthur at Starfish
Picture research Veena Holkar
Cartoons David Lock
Illustrations Cedric Knight, Peter Joyce

ISBN 1-899888-64-0
PN 5 4 3 2 1

© Chancerel International Publishers 2000

Produced by
Chancerel International Publishers
120 Long Acre
London
WC2E 9PA

Printed in Italy

Acknowledgements

T = top   B = below   C = centre   L = left   R = right

Cover: Photos: ©Mark Farrell; BP Amoco plc.; Gmi (Foster and Partner)
Diane Abbott, MP, 21BL; All England Lawn Tennis and Croquet Club, Wimbledon 25BL; Allsport 63BL, Photographer Mike Cooper 24TR, Simon Bruty 60BL, Adrian Murrell 61T, Pascal Rondeau 62TR, 63CL, Chris Cole 63CR; Alton Towers 83TR; Anthony Blake Photo Library 44TR/Photographer Gerrit Buntrock 44B, Andy Collison 45T; © Photo courtesy of Apple Computer, Inc 13B; Associated Press Ltd. 19T; Automobile Association 68T; Bath Archaeological Trust 8B; Bath Tourism Bureau 80C; Paul Balwin July 8, 1999 Needles in Asda bread, 103L; Bayeux Tapestry 12T; © BBC 52T, 52B, 56TL; The Big Issue 35CR; Blackpool Tourism Department 26TL; Blockbuster video 57TR; The Body Shop 58CR; Brewers and Licensed Retailers Association 64BL; Britain on View (BTA) 16T, 39T, 80T, Adam Woolfitt 80BR; The British Film Institute 50B, 51T, 51C; © The British Library *Royal 15 E.IV-f.236* 9B, *Royal 17.D.VI-f.93ᵛ* 12B; © The British Museum 8T, 9T, 9C, *The Royall Oake of Brittayne* 1649 11T, Francis Bacon 13T, *A voluptuary under the horrors of digestion 1792*, Gillray 17C; British Petroleum 43CL; Cadbury 23TR; Canary Wharf 79BC; Capital Radio 57B; Central Independent Television 17B; Photographer A. Burch 33BR, 35TR, 38TR, 70B, Jan Chipps 6CL, 18T (x3), 31B, 37T, 38B, 40B, 45CR, 46T, 56TR, 69CR, 75TL, 75BL, 77TL, 84T, 86T, 90, 91, 92LB, 94 (x4), Veena Holkar 32C, 33CL, 54BL, 59B, 62TL, 64TL, 64CR (x2), 65TL, 65TC, 65TR, 65BL, 65BR, 66BL, 77B, 79TR, H. Holtkamp 33TR, D. Prowse 4T, 14T, 20T, 25TL, 27BR, 54TR, 55TR, 57TC, 69CL, 74TR, 84B; Collections/Brian Shuel 23L, 24TL, 26BL; Colorific! 21C; Sylvia Cordaiy Photo Library Ltd 92 (x3); Cornwall Tourist Board 81B; Department of Transport 69T; Dewynters 47B; Edinburgh Festival Fringe/Programme cover design Gareth Rychter 85TR © 1999 Edinburgh International Festival 93; English Heritage 64TR, 81T; © European Passenger Services/Photographer Brian Newton 71BL, Peter Alvey 71BR; The Financial Times Business Enterprises Ltd 21CR; The Flag Institute 5 (x5), 88T (x2); The Flying Squad 49 (x3); The Football Association 24BL; Fortean Picture Library 85B; Melanie Friend/Format 28B, 48T; Sally Giles 34TL; Glaxo Holdings 40T, 43TR; GMPTE 67C; GMTV 62BL; Granada Television 53B, 56B; © Judy Harrison/Format 28BL; Harrods 59T; Crown Copyright. © Highbury Grove school, London; Historic Royal Palaces 16B, 111; Crown copyright is reproduced with the permission of the Controller of HMSO; Anthony Hopkins/Conway Vangelde 47TL; Hulton Deutsch 34B, 60T; Intercity East Coast 70C; Ironbridge Gorge Museum 82B; ITN 21TR; Richard Kalina/Shakespeare's Globe 50T; Lewes City Council 74BL; Life File/Photographer Emma Lee 28T, Andrew Ward 29TR, 32TL, 32BR, Nicola Sutton 41T, R.V. Johnson 73T, Juliet Highet 81CR; LIFFE 42B; London City Airport 31T;

London Transport Museum 20B, 66C, 66T, 67T; Manchester City Council 82T; The Mansell Collection Limited 5BR, 5TR, 11B, 76B, 76C; The Maritime Trust 79BR; Marks & Spencer 39B, 58TR; McDonalds 45C (x2); Jim Meads 7BR; The Metropolitan Police 6BL; MOMI Museum 78L: Marilyn Monroe © UIP/Captain Scarlet © ITC Entertainment Group Ltd/Muppets © Henson Associates, Inc; John Morrison 63T, 72CL, 75BR; National Express 69B (x2); National Gallery of Ireland 5TL, *Saint Patrick lighting the Paschal fir on the hill of the Slane* by Michael Healy; National Gallery, London *Saint George and the dragon* by Paolo Uccello 5BL; National Portrait Gallery *Sir William Pitt addressing the House of Commons* 15T; The National Trust Photographic Library/Photographer Mike Caldwell 72CL, Nick Meers 73C, Joe Cornish 74CL; Natural History Museum 78TR; Nissan 83CR; Northern Ireland Tourist Board 89 (x4); © Joanne O'Brien/Format 88B; Oxfam 58CL; Oxford Cartographers cover; Raissa Page/Format 58B; Polygram Film International 46B; The Post Office 7BL, 51B, 71TL; Press Association 6TR, 8BR, 14B; Quad Electroacoustics 43CR; Radio 1/Rufus Leonard Design Consultants 57BL; Road Alert! 68B, Photographer Alex MacNaughton 74BR; Robert Harding Picture Library/Photographer Adam Woolfitt 47C, Walter Rawlings 79BR, Royal Botanic Gardens, Kew 79TL; Royal Mint/© Lord Chamberlain's Office, Buckingham Palace 10T; Royal Society for the Prevention of Accidents 27BL; Rugby Football Club 61C; Sainsbury's 42T, 58CR; The Savoy group of hotels and restaurants/The Berkeley 44TL; The Science Photo Library 67B; Scottish Tourist Board 84C, 85TL; © C. Seddons/CIWF 75TR; Shout/© D.C.Thomson & Co. Ltd. 55BR; Heinz Sill 25TR; Smash Hits 55BCL; The Snowdon Mountain Railway 87C; Spectrum Colour Library 7C, 76T; Steel Hunter Limited 43CT; Stena Sealink/Chameleon Design Consultancy 30T; Claudio Steuer 81TL; Still Moving Picture Company 22L, 85C; Stone's Restaurant 45B; © Sugar Ltd 1999 55LB; Colin Taylor Productions 27TL; Ms Emma Thompson 47TR; © TRMC/Railcard 71TR; TRMC/Photographer Alan Cheek 70TR; TV HITS 55BCR; University of Birmingham 38C; Vintage Books 21CL; Virgin Management Ltd 43BL; Virgin Radio 57BR; Wales Tourist Board 72TR, 86B, 87T, 87B; John Walmsley Photo-Library 36B, 37BL, 37BR, 54BR; Wedgwood 83B; Which? Consumers' Association/Photograph Steve Bielschowsky 30B; Mo Wilson/Format 29B; Susan Wilson 18B; Woburn Abbey by kind permission of the Marquess of Tavistock and the Trustees of the Bedford Estate 10B; Youth Exchange Centre 19C; Benjamin Zephaniah/Sandra Boyce Management for poem and photo 53T.

Every effort has been made to contact the copyright holders of material used in this book. The publishers apologise for any omissions and will be pleased to make the necessary arrangement when the title is reprinted.

CONTENTS

Cambridge Language
and
Activity Courses

The British Isles

1 **a** Try and draw a map of the British Isles from memory.
b Compare your map with a map of the British Isles.

On British passports the country is called the United Kingdom of Great Britain and Northern Ireland.

One country?

The British Isles is the name for a collection of about 4,000 islands, including Great Britain and Ireland. The name, the British Isles, is usually only seen on maps.

Great Britain, known as Britain, or GB, is the name for the largest of the islands. It includes England, Scotland and Wales, but it does not include Northern Ireland or the Republic of Ireland. You see the abbreviation GB on driving licences of people who live in England, Scotland and Wales.

The United Kingdom, or the UK, is a political term, which includes England, Scotland, Wales and Northern Ireland. All of these countries are represented in Parliament in London and the abbreviation UK is used on most official documents produced by Parliament. Now Scotland and Wales have their own local parliaments, with power to make decisions about their countries.

Everybody from the UK is British, but be careful: only people from England are English. People from Wales think of themselves as Welsh; people from Scotland as Scottish; people from Northern Ireland as either British or Irish.

What's a county?

Britain is split up into counties. The word county describes an area with its own local government. County councils are elected to run things, such as education, housing, town planning and rubbish disposal. They look after roads, libraries and swimming pools.

Many counties, like Yorkshire, Berkshire and Lancashire, contain the word *shire*, which is an old word for county. In writing, it is usual to abbreviate names of counties containing the word *shire*: Lancashire becomes Lancs; Wiltshire becomes Wilts; South Yorkshire becomes S. Yorks.

2 True or false? Correct the sentences that are false.
   a If you hold a British passport, you are from England, Scotland, Wales or Northern Ireland.
   b Someone from Scotland can represent GB in the Olympic Games.
   c A person from the Republic of Ireland is British.

3 Look at the map of the British Isles. True or false? Correct the sentences that are false.
   a The capital of Wales is Swansea.
   b The capital of Northern Ireland is Belfast.
   c It is more mountainous in the south than in the north of Britain.
   d The highest mountain in England is Ben Nevis.
   e The river which runs through Oxford and London is the Thames.

4 Copy and complete the sentences.
   a London is in the ...-east of Britain.
   b Birmingham is ... of London, in a part of Britain called the Midlands.
   c Bristol is in the ...-west of Britain.

5 What is your country's equivalent of a county?

6 **a** Which country in the British Isles is not represented on the Union Jack?
   b Draw the flag of your country. What does it represent?
   c Describe one of the paintings on page 5. What is happening?
   d Who is the patron saint of your country? Why is s/he famous?

Flags and saints

The Saint Andrew's cross is the Scottish flag. Saint Andrew, a fisherman, was one of the 12 apostles who followed Jesus Christ. Paintings of Saint Andrew often show him being killed on an X-shaped cross. Saint Andrew's Day is celebrated on 30 November. He is the patron saint of both Scotland and Russia.

The Saint Patrick's cross is the former flag of Ireland. Saint Patrick is the patron saint of Ireland. He was born about AD 390. He converted the Irish to Christianity and is supposed to have got rid of all the snakes in Ireland. Saint Patrick's Day is celebrated on 17 March.

The British flag, known as the Union Jack, is a combination of three flags: the Saint Andrew's cross, the Saint Patrick's cross and the Saint George's cross.

The Saint George's cross is the English flag. Saint George is the patron saint of England. He was a soldier famous for saving a princess from being eaten by a dragon. George wounded the dragon and took it back to the city of Silene, Libya, on a lead like a dog. Saint George's Day is celebrated on 23 April. Saint George is also the patron saint of Germany, Portugal and Greece.

The Welsh flag shows a dragon. Saint David, the patron saint of Wales, started a number of monasteries in the country. Paintings of Saint David normally show him with a dove on his shoulder. His relics are now in Saint David's Cathedral in Wales. Saint David's Day is celebrated on 1 March.

Very British

1 **a** Think of four things that you think are typically British.
b Compare your list with the typically British things mentioned in the text.

Hooligans

The British are polite ...

... most of the time!

Most British people expect the person in front of them to hold the door open for them. People think you are rude, if you do not do this. But British football supporters have a reputation for violence.

Queues

The British prefer to queue ...

... usually!

Most British people queue when they are waiting for a bus or waiting to be served in a shop. Things are different during the rush hour. When a bus or train arrives, people often push forward to make sure they get on. This is called jumping the queue.

The police

The British police are wonderful ...

... generally speaking.

You can ask a police officer for help, if you are lost. Most British police officers are friendly, helpful and polite. But sometimes the police have been accused of not treating people fairly, especially people from black and Asian communities.

The cold

British people are used to the cold. They use thick curtains and carpets to keep their houses warm. A lot of British houses are old and not always well insulated. British people must pay VAT on all gas and electricity, so heating costs are high. Some people can't afford to heat their homes well. Every winter about 350 old people die of hypothermia, extreme loss of body heat.

Britain is cold ...

Pollution

Britain is sometimes foggy in winter, but it does not have the kind of smog it used to have. Smog was smoke from coal mixing with fog to pollute the air. In 1956, smokeless zones were created in towns and cities and the amount of industrial smoke from factories was limited by law. The air in cities became much cleaner.

Now there are so many fumes from cars, lorries and buses that air quality is not very good. The Government says it will try to stop car drivers from using their cars so much and improve public transport.

Britain is not a very foggy country, but there is a lot of air pollution caused by traffic.

Animals

The British celebrate the 150th anniversary of the RSPCA by printing special stamps ...

... but they still go fox-hunting.

The British love animals so much that there is a *Royal* Society for the Prevention of Cruelty to Animals (RSPCA), but only a *National* Society for the Prevention of Cruelty to Children (NSPCC). Fox-hunting has been a British tradition for hundreds of years. Specially trained dogs hunt a fox, with men and women following on horseback. The fox is often killed by the dogs.

2 Make a list of things that you think are typical of your country. Does your partner agree with you or not? Why?

IDENTITY Influences

1 a Britain was invaded by many different peoples in early times.
Has your country ever been invaded? If yes, when?
b Look at the map. Where did Britain's invaders come from?
2 Read the text to find out if you are right.

The Celts

Between the sixth and the third century BC, the British Isles were invaded by Celtic tribes, who settled in southern England. They originally came from central Europe. Their culture goes back to about 1200 BC. Between 500 and 250 BC, they were the most powerful people north of the Alps. They were pagan, with priests known as Druids, but later converted to Christianity. It was Celtic missionaries who spread the Christian religion through Scotland and northern England.

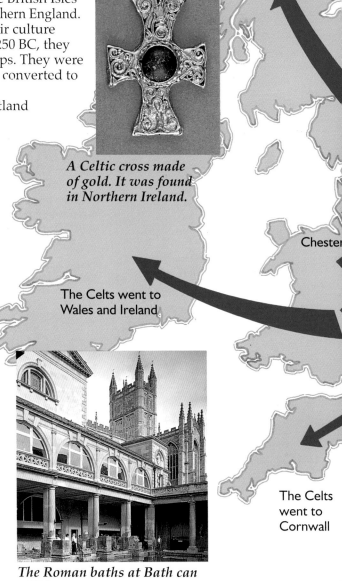

The Celts went to Scotland

A Celtic cross made of gold. It was found in Northern Ireland.

Chester

The Celts went to Wales and Ireland

The Celts went to Cornwall

The Romans

In AD 43, the Romans invaded southern Britain. It became a Roman colony called *Britannia*. The Romans set up their capital in London and built major cities in Bath, Chester and York. The cities contained beautiful buildings, squares and public baths. Fine villas were built for Celtic aristocrats who accepted Roman rule.

The Roman invasion was not completely peaceful. In AD 60, the Iceni, a tribe led by Queen Boudicca, destroyed three cities, including London. The Romans stopped the rebellion brutally and Boudicca killed herself.

The tribes of Scotland never completely surrendered to the Romans. As a result, in AD 122, Emperor Hadrian built a long wall to defend the border between England and Scotland. Hadrian's Wall was overrun several times by Scottish tribes and was finally abandoned in AD 383. By then, the Roman Empire was collapsing and the Roman legions had left Britain to fight the tribes on the continent.

The Roman baths at Bath can still be seen.

The Saxons, Jutes and Angles

From about AD 350, Germanic tribes began invading south-east England. The tribes came from what is now northern Germany, Holland and Denmark. The first to come were the Saxons, joined later by the Jutes and Angles. The Angles gave England its name. Britain had the protection of only a few Roman legions. The native people could not stop the new enemy, known as the Anglo-Saxons. The Celts fled north and west taking their ancient arts and languages with them. Celtic languages have disappeared from most of Europe, but are still spoken in parts of Wales, Ireland and Scotland. Celtic Christians later returned to England from Scotland and Ireland as missionaries. The Anglo-Saxons in southern England were converted to Christianity following the arrival of Saint Augustine of Rome in AD 597. As Christianity spread, churches and monasteries were built all over England.

A helmet found in the burial ship of an Anglo-Saxon king at Sutton Hoo in the south of England.

The Vikings came from Scandinavia

ian's Wall

This coin, found near York, shows King Cnut.

The Vikings

About AD 790, the Vikings started to invade England. The Norsemen, who came from Norway, mainly settled in Scotland and Ireland. The north and east of England were settled by the Danes. The Vikings were excellent traders and navigators. They traded in silk and furs as far as Russia. In 1016, England became part of the Scandinavian empire under King Cnut. By 1066, England was again facing invasion from the north and the south. In September, King Harold II marched north to defeat his half-brother, the king of Norway, at the Battle of Stamford Bridge. Just three weeks later, he himself was defeated and killed at Hastings by another invader of Viking origin, William, Duke of Normandy, from northern France.

The Anglo-Saxons came from Germany, Holland and Denmark

London ■

The Romans came from Italy

The Normans

The Duke of Normandy, known as William the Conqueror, now became King of England, establishing a new Anglo-Norman state. England became a strong, centralised country under military rule. The Normans built castles all over England to control England better. William was a harsh ruler: he destroyed many villages to make sure the English people did not rebel. Norman power was absolute, and the language of the new rulers, Norman French, had a lasting effect on English. Since 1066, England has never been invaded.

The Normans came from Scandinavia, via northern France

William of Normandy was crowned King William I in London on Christmas Day, 1066.

3 | How did each invasion change Britain?

IDENTITY Empire

1 Read the text to find out about the following.
a Why Britain is a Protestant country.
b The move towards parliamentary democracy.
c The rise and fall of the British Empire.

Henry VIII and the Church

King Henry VIII (1491–1547) is famous for his six wives and his ambitions. He married Catherine of Aragon, niece of Emperor Charles V, who was ruler of most of Europe and the Americas. They had a daughter but not the son and heir Henry wanted. Henry asked the Pope for a divorce from Catherine, when his mistress, Anne Boleyn, became pregnant. The Pope did not answer, so Henry made the Archbishop of Canterbury give him a divorce. Henry made the Catholic Church in England independent of Rome. Parliament's Act of Supremacy in 1534 made the king Head of the Church of England, which became Protestant. This was popular with many English people who were already Protestant.

Queen Elizabeth II still has the title **Fidei Defensor** *today. The abbreviation* **FD** *appears on every British coin.*

The Pope had given the title *Fidei Defensor*, Defender of Faith, to King Henry VIII. Henry kept this title, when he created the Church of England.

Henry's second daughter, Elizabeth I, became one of England's greatest monarchs. During her reign (1558–1603), England's sailors captured many Spanish ships bringing treasure from the Americas. King Philip of Spain, encouraged by the Pope, who wanted to restore Catholicism to England, sent the Spanish Armada. This fleet of 130 ships went to invade England in 1588, but it was defeated. England became the most important Protestant power in Europe.

2 a Look at the background of the painting. What do you think is happening?
b What is Elizabeth I holding in her right hand. Why?

George Gower's **Armada Portrait** *shows Queen Elizabeth I and the defeat of the Spanish Armada.*

The rise of Parliament

King Charles I (1600–1649) believed that the monarch was appointed by God to rule and had absolute power. The elected English Parliament disagreed. The result was the Civil War, leading to the execution of the king in 1649. For the next 11 years, England was a republic, though Oliver Cromwell, the parliamentary leader and most important man in England, took more and more power until he himself became a dictator.

After his death, Parliament asked the executed king's son to return to England. In spite of this, there was no return to the absolute rule of kings and no future monarch would ever seriously challenge the power of Parliament.

Cromwell destroying the monarchy. The monarchy is shown as "The Royall Oake".

Empire and industry

In 1833, it became illegal to employ children under the age of 13 for more than 48 hours per week.

During the eighteenth and nineteenth centuries, Britain itself was peaceful. Abroad, it was aggressively expanding its empire. It became a powerful and rich country because of its empire and its industry. Cheap raw materials, produced by badly paid or unpaid workers, were imported from the colonies. The technological changes of the Industrial Revolution allowed Britain to manufacture products cheaply for export back to the colonies and other countries.

The Industrial Revolution caused great social changes in Britain. Many people moved from the land to the cities. These people worked in the factories, creating an urban working class, which was often very poor. In Queen Victoria's reign (1837–1901), children as young as four had jobs in factories and mines. Their parents had no right to vote and try to change things.

The Reform Act of 1832 gave the vote to all men who owned a house, but it was not until 1918 that the right to vote was given to all men over 21 and to women over 30. Women under 30 had to wait until 1928 for the vote.

Britain at its most powerful had colonies in every continent, but the end of the Empire came quickly, after the Second World War (1939–1945). India, one of the most important colonies, became independent in 1948. In the 1960s, the African and Caribbean countries also became independent. British people began to realise that their country was no longer an imperial world power but just a country in Europe.

3 **a** Did your country ever have any overseas colonies?
   b When were women given the vote in your country? Did this happen sooner or later than in Britain?

4 **a** Choose one of the following dates and give a short description of what happened in Britain: 1534, 1588, 1649, 1833, 1948.
   b What was happening in your country at the same time?

IDENTITY In English

1 The English language has a lot of words because it is a mixture of many languages. Read the text to find out if your own language is linked to English. If yes, how is it linked?

The Germanic influence

The Bayeux Tapestry shows the Normans invading England. Before they invaded, the language of England was mainly Germanic Old English.

The Anglo-Saxons, who invaded England in AD 350, came from Germany, Denmark and Holland. They spoke a Germanic language which became the basis of Old English. Even today, words used in modern English for everyday life are mostly Anglo-Saxon, or Germanic, in origin. Germanic languages, such as Danish, German, Norwegian and Swedish, have very similar words for the expressions in the box below. Words of Germanic origin are usually short (often just one syllable) and tend to be informal in modern English.

> shoe clothes earth sun moon day man
> wife child friend house food water
> sleep love say live have be work

The French influence

English also has many similarities with Romance languages, whose origin is Latin. The words in the box below came to England with the French-speaking Normans. Notice that the words are associated with power: Norman French was used as the language of government. Words of Latin origin are usually longer than words of Germanic origin and often have a more formal meaning in English than in the original Romance language.

> government parliament judge
> court legal military army
> crown nation state country
> power authority people

Norman French words did not enter English immediately. When the Normans invaded in 1066, ordinary people still spoke Old English.

Imagine a Norman feast. The English would look after the animals and cook the meat, still calling the animals by their Old English names. The Normans, when they saw the cooked meat arrive at the table, would use French ones. This explains why the English language now has different words for animals and meats.

ANIMAL		MEAT	
Anglo-Saxon	**Modern English**	**French**	**Modern English**
pigga	pig	*porc*	pork
scep	sheep	*mouton*	mutton
cu	cow	*boeuf*	beef

In the fourteenth century, a new form of English was used: Middle English, which was Old English enriched by thousands of French words. The fourteenth-century poet, Chaucer (right), wrote in Middle English.

The classical influence

The Renaissance came two centuries later. It was a revival of interest in ancient Greek and Roman culture. Some words from Latin had already come into English through Norman French. Now thousands more words of Latin origin flooded into English. This explains why modern English has pairs of words which mean almost the same thing, such as *base*, which came into English from Norman French, and *basis*, which came into English during the Renaissance. Hundreds of Greek words also appeared in English.

At the same time, it became more popular throughout Europe for people to use their mother tongue, not Latin, for written documents. They were especially interested in reading the Bible in their own language. By the seventeenth century, it was possible to describe something in English with words of Germanic, Latin and Greek origin. This is still true today. Compare the following:

GERMANIC	LATIN	GREEK
book	**libr**ary	**biblio**graphy
re**new**	re**no**vate	**neo**lithic
water	**aqua**tic	**hydr**aulic

The seventeenth-century writer, Francis Bacon (above), wrote either in Latin or in modern English.

A world language

Words from other cultures and countries came into English as a result of trade and colonial expansion: *alcohol* and *algebra* came from Arabic; *divan* and *khaki* from Persian; *chocolate* and *tomato* from native American languages; *bungalow* and *cot* from Gujerati; *tea* and *tycoon* from Chinese.

The period from the Renaissance to the present day has also seen many new ideas and inventions, especially in science and technology. As new things are invented, new words have to be created. Often these words are created from existing Greek or Latin words put together in new ways. When someone invented an instrument for speaking to another person at a distance, it was called a *telephone*, from the Greek words *tele* (= far) and *phone* (= sound). There are now thousands of such words in English. Just think of *television*, *video*, *microscope*, *psychology* and *thermometer*.

Other words were invented in the English-speaking former colonies, the USA in particular. Many British people complain about Americanisms entering the English language, but do not realise how many of the words they already use come from American English. It is because of the USA that English is now truly a world language. Over 90 per cent of scientific papers are written in English and many people who do not speak each other's mother tongue are most likely to communicate in English.

Nowadays the importance of computer software, often invented in America, spreads the English language worldwide.

2　**a** Have any English words entered your own language in recent years?
　b Do English words in your language have an English pronunciation?

1 **a** How many chambers are there in your Parliament and what are they called?
b How old do you have to be to vote in your country?
c How many political parties are there in your country and what are they called?
d What is the title of the most powerful person in Parliament in your country?

Parliament

The British Parliament has two houses, or chambers: the House of Commons and the House of Lords. The House of Commons is the most powerful and decides national policy, but the House of Lords can ask the House of Commons to rewrite certain parts of a bill before it becomes a new law.

The House of Commons consists of Members of Parliament, MPs. Each MP is elected by voters in one constituency (region). There are 659 MPs, or seats, in the House of Commons. In 1994, there were only 59 women MPs. This number increased to 101 when the Labour Party took office in 1997.

Until 1999 there were 1,213 members of the House of Lords, including 646 hereditary peers, whose titles are inherited. There were also a number of judges and bishops. But most members were life peers, who hold their titles for their lifetime only. Often, life peers are politicians who were members of the House of Commons in the past.

The Labour Government of Tony Blair promised to reform the House of Lords and make it an elected House. But how the elections will work is still being debated. In the meantime, the number of hereditary peers has been reduced to 92 Lords. The other hereditary peers have kept their titles but can no longer attend or vote in Parliament.

The House of Commons and the House of Lords meet in the Houses of Parliament, more commonly known as Westminster. The clock tower of the Houses of Parliament is called Big Ben.

Forming a government

The party with most MPs forms the Government. The leader of the winning party automatically becomes Prime Minister and appoints the Cabinet. The members of the Cabinet are the leading government ministers. The Prime Minister is the most important person in Parliament (Britain does not have a president). The party which comes second is the Opposition and forms its own Shadow Cabinet.

British Prime Ministers have lived at 10 Downing Street since 1731. The Chancellor of the Exchequer (responsible for money and finance) lives next door at number 11. People often talk about "Downing Street" when they mean the Prime Minister and his or her Cabinet.

A policeman guarding 10 Downing Street. The Prime Minister and the Cabinet meet here almost every week. Together they run the country.

Two-party politics

Since the eighteenth century, the two main parties have sat facing each other in the House of Commons. Sitting on the front benches are the leading members of the government. Opposite them sit the most important members of the main opposition party. The House of Commons still looks almost the same today.

Every five years, British people over the age of 18 can vote in a general election. People vote for the candidate they want in their constituency (region). The candidate who wins becomes the MP in the House of Commons, even if he or she gets only one vote more than the candidate who is second. This is called the first-past-the-post system. The first-past-the-post electoral system in Britain usually makes two parties powerful, while smaller parties do not have many MPs. Since the 1920s, the two main parties have been the left-wing Labour Party and the right-wing Conservative Party.

The Liberal Democrats are not happy with the first-past-the-post electoral system. This is because it is a party, which does not win many seats in Parliament, but comes second in many constituencies. It would prefer a system of proportional representation, in which the number of MPs is based on the number of people who vote for a party in the whole of the country. When British people vote in European Union elections, there is a proportional representation system.

2. Draw a diagram of the most important chamber in your country. Is it a semi-circle? Compare it with the shape of the House of Commons.

3. a Compare the percentage of Liberal Democrat MPs with the percentage of people that voted for them. How many Liberal Democrat MPs would there be in the House of Commons, if Britain had a system of proportional representation?
   b What electoral system does your country have?

4. Answer Question 1 about Britain. Make a list of the differences between your country and Britain.

THE EFFECTS OF THE FIRST-PAST-THE-POST ELECTORAL SYSTEM

Britain's electoral system gives small political parties very few MPs in the House of Commons, even though they may get many votes.

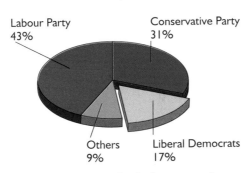

Labour Party 43%
Conservative Party 31%
Others 9%
Liberal Democrats 17%

Percentage of votes in the last general election.

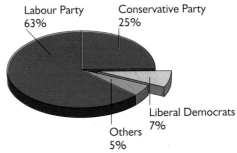

Labour Party 63%
Conservative Party 25%
Liberal Democrats 7%
Others 5%

Percentage of MPs in the House of Commons after the last general election.

The Monarchy

1 **a** Who is the head of state in your country?
b Find out which countries in Europe have a monarchy.
c Make a list of three things you think a king or queen should do.

What does the Queen do?

The Queen at the State Opening of Parliament. When a bill has been passed by Parliament it goes to her for Royal Assent before it becomes law. She could refuse to sign it, but she never does. The Royal Assent has not been refused since 1707.

Britain is a constitutional monarchy. This means that the monarch, at the moment Queen Elizabeth II, is the head of state. The Queen is also the head of the judiciary (all the judges) and of the Church of England, as well as the Commander-in-Chief of the armed forces. Her face is on all British bank notes, coins and postage stamps.

The Queen's constitutional role is mainly symbolic. True power lies with the Prime Minister and his or her Cabinet. When the Queen formally opens Parliament every autumn, the speech she makes from the throne, giving details of the Government's future plans, is written for her by politicians. Nothing becomes British law without the monarch's signature, but the Queen would never refuse to sign a bill, which has been passed by Parliament. Officially the Queen appoints the Prime Minister, but traditionally she always asks the leader of the party with a majority in the House of Commons.

Representing Britain

The most important function of the Queen is ceremonial. On great occasions, such as the State Opening of Parliament, she is driven through the streets in a golden carriage, guarded by soldiers. She gives a state banquet, usually in her home at Buckingham Palace, when foreign monarchs or heads of state visit Britain. Soldiers dressed in eighteenth-century uniforms help her to welcome them.

The Queen is head of the Commonwealth (a group of former and present-day British colonies). As head of the Commonwealth, she meets and entertains the prime ministers of the member states.

Since Elizabeth II came to the throne in 1952, she has represented Britain on visits to most parts of the world. Prime Ministers come and go, but she carries on above politics, a symbol of British traditions.

This is the Queen's crown. She only wears it for state occasions. On the front of the crown is the biggest diamond in the world, which is from India.

An ideal British family? 🎧

The surname of the royal family is Windsor. This might sound very British, but the royal family's ancestors were German. The Queen's great-great-grandmother, Queen Victoria (1819–1910), was born in Britain, but her mother and her husband were both German. When Queen Victoria got married, she became a Saxe-Coburg-Gotha.

The British royal family continued with this surname until the First World War (1914–1918) when King George V (1865–1936) decided to take a more English-sounding name. He chose Windsor, which is the name of one of the royal castles.

King George VI and Queen Elizabeth (now known as the Queen Mother) became very popular with the British people during the Second World War (1939–1945). They stayed in London, even though their home, Buckingham Palace, was bombed.

In 1953, millions of people watched Queen Elizabeth II's coronation on television and thought of her, her husband and their first two little children as an ideal British family. This image of royal family did not last.

Recent problems for members of the royal family have had a great effect on their popularity. Three of the Queen's children have divorced. The Queen's youngest son, Edward, waited until he was 35 to get married, because he wanted to make sure his marriage would work. Newspapers and magazines publish information and photographs of the private lives of the royal family.

Royal scandals are not a twentieth-century invention. King George IV (1762–1830) was criticised for his mistresses, overeating, drinking and gambling. Another king, Edward VII (1841–1910), openly kept a number of mistresses and was involved in a gambling scandal.

The present royal family is criticised, because it does not seem to show emotions easily, especially when Diana, Princess of Wales, died suddenly in a car crash in 1997. British people show less respect for the royal family: most still want a monarchy, but expect the royal family to modernise, earn its money and set an example.

A caricature of King George IV after a heavy meal in 1792.

◄ *Queen Elizabeth II with her husband Prince Philip and their dogs, as seen on a satirical television programme.*

2 **a** Do you think a royal family should set an example?

b Look at the caricatures of the present royal family and King George IV in 1792. Should the media show the royal family in this way?

c Does your country have a monarchy? If not, would you like to have a monarchy?

d Do you think the idea of a monarchy is out of date?

1 a Which of the countries in the box on the right are members of the European Union (EU)?
b Which of the countries in the box on the right are members of the Commonwealth?
c Which country(ies) is/are member(s) of neither?
2 Read the text to find out if you are right.

Australia	Germany	Nigeria
Austria	China	Sweden
Denmark	India	South Africa
Finland	Italy	USA

Britain and the Commonwealth

Hi! My name's Bruce O'Hallahan. I'm from Australia. Because I'm under 27, I can spend up to two years working in Britain. That'll pay for my holiday in Europe!

Hello. My name is Abida Chattopadhyay. I live in India. I hope to get a scholarship from the Commonwealth so that I can study medicine at a British university.

Hi! My name is Obi Onenyi and I'm from Nigeria. I want to run for Nigeria in the next Commonwealth Games. Last time, Nigeria won 11 gold medals.

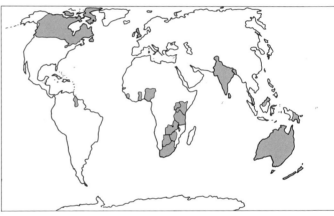

The Commonwealth is a group of former British colonies, together with six countries which are still British.

Because it is an island, Britain has always been forced to trade with other countries. During the nineteenth century, Britain traded all over the world and had a large empire overseas. The Commonwealth is an association of the ex-colonies in the Empire and works to encourage cultural relations between members. South Africa was forced to leave the Commonwealth in 1961 because of apartheid. In 1994, after "one person, one vote" elections, South Africa rejoined the Commonwealth.

The members of the Commonwealth have many different styles of government. Some of the countries, such as Canada, Australia and New Zealand recognise the Queen as their head of state. Others, such as India, are republics, and choose their own heads of state. In a referendum held in 1999 Australia decided to remain a constitutional monarchy rather than become a republic. All of the countries recognise the Queen as head of the Commonwealth, though some countries feel there should be an elected leader.

Voting in the 1994 South African elections.

Britain and America 🎧

Britain and the USA were allies in both World Wars and in the Korean War, and for many years they had what was called "a special relationship". In recent years, however, they have not always supported each other. The USA did not help Britain and France during the Suez crisis in 1956. Britain did not support the USA in the 1964–73 Vietnam War. In the Gulf War in 1991 and the Kosovo crisis (1999), however, the American and British military forces worked together.

Churchill from Britain (left) meets Roosevelt from the USA in 1945. On the right is Stalin from the USSR.

Britain and Europe 🎧

Britain's most important relationship today is with the European Union (EU). At first, when the Common Market (the original name for the EU) was set up in 1957, Britain was not keen to join. By 1963, Britain realised that it had to become a member nation, but its application was not accepted. It was only in 1973 that Britain was allowed to join.

Now over half of Britain's trade is with the European Union. Even so, not all British people are sure that Europe is a good thing for Britain. About half of British people believe that Britain needs Europe because it offers British companies a market of over 350 million people.

British membership of the EU has always been controversial. There was much political debate about whether Britain should join the single European currency. The Government decided that it would not join at first, but would wait and join later.

To learn more about other EU countries young people from the UK go on exchange visits. The European Union funds the Youth Exchange Centre. The young people must organise the trip and raise some of the money for the exchange themselves. Under the Erasmus programme, university students go and study in other EU countries. The EU gives them a small grant to help with their expenses.

This youth group from Bradford organised a meeting with the local mayor for their German exchange partners.

3 True or false? Correct the sentences that are false.
   a Britain has links with countries in all of the five continents.
   b The Commonwealth is the most important relationship for Britain today.
   c The majority of people in Britain are in favour of Europe.

4 a Find reasons in the text why countries are part of groups such as the EU or the Commonwealth. Do you think they are good reasons?
   b Is your country a member of the EU? Do you think this is a good idea?

Answers to **1a**: Austria, Denmark, Finland, Germany, Italy, Sweden. **1b**: Australia, India, Nigeria, South Africa. **1c**: USA, China.

19

Being British

A cosmopolitan society

Most people in Britain are English, Scottish or Welsh, but in some cities you can meet people of many different nationalities. In London you will find lots of businesses run by Arabs, Greeks, Indians, Italians, Jamaicans, Nigerians, Portuguese, Spanish, Turkish, as well as British.

But is Britain a cosmopolitan society? It really depends on where you go. There are large areas of Britain untouched by immigration. In the last census, 5.5 per cent of the 57 million population described themselves as belonging to an ethnic minority of Caribbean, African or Asian origin. In Scotland, Wales, the North and the South West of England, only 1 per cent of the population belongs to an ethnic minority. Most members of ethnic minorities live in the South East. In Greater London, they represent 20 per cent of the population.

London's immigrants come from inside and outside Europe. Many people from the EU come to work for a short time. There is almost the same number of Irish immigrants (3.8 per cent of the population) as Caribbean immigrants (4.4 per cent of the population). Many so-called "immigrants" are born in Britain: more than 36,000 Londoners born in Britain describe themselves as "Black British" instead of "African" or "Afro-Caribbean".

This building in London was first a French Protestant church, then a synagogue and is now a mosque.

A tradition of immigration

People have been coming to Britain for centuries: some to get a better life, some to escape natural disasters, some as political or religious refugees. Many Irish people came to England in 1845 to escape famine. Many more came simply to find work. Most of the roads, railways and canals built in the nineteenth century were made by Irish workers.

The greatest wave of immigration was in the 1950s and 1960s. This happened not only in Britain but also throughout Western Europe. Many companies needed people for unskilled or semi-skilled jobs. Britain advertised, particularly in the English-speaking islands of the Caribbean, for people to come to Britain and work. Other people came from Pakistan, Bangladesh, India and Hong Kong.

Many people came to Britain in the 1950s to work in hospitals, on the buses or for the railways.

A multiracial society 🎧

Britain has not yet solved the problems of a multiracial society.
The number of people asking to settle in Britain is rising, but
Britain, since 1971, has reduced the number of people coming
from outside Europe, which it allows to stay.

In spite of anti-racist laws, some people in Britain blame
unemployment and poor housing on "immigrants". By this,
they mean people whose skin colour is different from their own.

Many members of ethnic minorities have overcome prejudice
and have achieved distinction in the media, in sport, in
commerce and in public life.

*Zeinab Badawi is a
TV news presenter.*

*Timothy Mo is a
well-known novelist.*

*Naomi Campbell is a
supermodel.*

*Sri and Gopi Hinduja are the
eighth-richest people in Britain.
They have interests in banking,
manufacturing and oil.*

Diane Abbott is an MP.

2 **a** Look at the photos. What do these people do?
   b Do you think it is easy to be successful in these jobs?
   c Give three examples of members of ethnic minorities
      who have achieved distinction in your country.
3 Imagine you live in London. Describe the street in which
   you live. Think about the following questions:
   a Where do you come from?
   b Where do your neighbours come from?
   c How long have you lived in London?
   d What do you do?
4 **a** How does immigration in Britain compare with that of
      your country?
   b What are reasons for immigration in your country?

The British year

JANUARY

New Year's Eve: all over Britain on 31 December there are New Year celebrations. Most people see in the New Year with friends and relations. At midnight on New Year's Eve, everybody joins hands and sings *Auld Lang Syne*, a poem by the Scottish poet Robert Burns. In Scotland and the North of England, people go first footing. They call at friends' houses, trying to be the first person through the door after midnight. To symbolise good luck, the visitor carries a piece of coal and a glass of water.

New Year's Day: on New Year's Day (1 January) people make New Year's resolutions. They decide to do something to improve their lives. For example, people decide to give up smoking or go to the gym once a week.

The luckiest type of first footer is a tall, dark man.

1 Describe how you usually celebrate New Year. Describe what you wear, what you eat, who you meet and what you do.

FEBRUARY

Crufts Dog Show: dog breeders from all over the world bring their valuable dogs to take part in Crufts Dog Show in Birmingham. There are prizes for most breeds and one for the best dog, who is given the title Crufts Supreme Champion.

Saint Valentine's Day: Saint Valentine's Day is 14 February. People send a Valentine's card to someone they love, fancy, admire or secretly like. Usually you don't sign your name. The person who receives the card has to guess who sent it.

A Valentine's card

> Roses are red
> Violets are blue
> Sugar is sweet
> And so are you

A traditional verse inside a Valentine's card.

2 a Would you send a Valentine's card? Who to?
b When do you send cards?

MARCH

The Boat Race: this rowing race between the universities of Oxford and Cambridge has been held on the River Thames in London almost every year since 1836. The length of the course is 4½ miles (7.2 kilometres).

Pancake Day: Pancake Day, or Shrove Tuesday, is the day before Lent starts. Lent is a Christian fast which lasts for 40 days before Easter. Pancake Day is traditionally a day of celebration, the last day that you can eat what you want until Easter. Pancakes are made of flour, eggs and milk: all things which should not be eaten during Lent. Nowadays people don't fast, but some people give up sweets or smoking.

This is a pancake race. Each competitor carries a pancake in a frying pan. While running, they have to throw the pancake in the air and catch it again in the pan. The competitors are usually women.

3 In many countries the equivalent of Pancake Day is Mardi Gras or Carnival. Does your country celebrate Pancake Day, Mardi Gras or Carnival? What do you do?

APRIL

April Fool's Day: April Fool's Day is 1 April. You can play jokes on people, even on teachers. When they discover the joke, you say, "April Fool!". You have to play the joke before 12 o'clock midday, otherwise the joke's on you.

Easter eggs are made of chocolate and usually wrapped in silver paper and bows.

Easter: schools close for two weeks at Easter. On Good Friday, people eat hot cross buns, which are small sweet rolls. They eat them toasted with butter. People give each other chocolate Easter eggs on Easter Sunday. The eggs are usually hollow and contain sweets.

The London Marathon: this is one of the biggest marathons in the world. Each year about 30,000 people start the race and about 25,000 finish. Some people take part to raise money for charity, often wearing costumes. There is also a race for people in wheelchairs.

4 How do you celebrate Easter? Describe what you wear, what you eat and who you meet.

MAY

May Day: in villages throughout Britain on 1 May you can see children dancing round the maypole and singing songs. It is a pagan festival to celebrate the end of winter and welcome summer.

FA (Football Association) Cup Final: this is the biggest day in the football calendar. Two English football clubs play to win the FA Cup. The match takes place at Wembley Stadium in London. Scotland has its own FA Cup Final, played at Hampden Park in Glasgow.

Chelsea Flower Show: this is Britain's most important flower and garden show. Thousands of people come to see the prize flowers and specially built gardens.

People celebrating May Day. The maypole is a symbol of fertility.

An FA Cup Final programme.

1. What do you do to celebrate the end of winter in your country? Compare this with Britain.

JUNE

It is traditional for men and women to go to the horse-racing at Ascot wearing their best hats.

Royal Ascot: this is one of the biggest horse-race meetings in Britain. It is held at Ascot, in the south of England. The Queen drives there from Windsor Castle. Ascot lasts for four days.

Trooping the Colour: this is the second Saturday in June and celebrates the Queen's official birthday (her real birthday is 21 April). She watches a parade of hundreds of soldiers. There is lots of marching, military music and the soldiers are dressed in colourful uniforms.

2. If you were in Britain in June, which event would you prefer to go to: Trooping the Colour or Royal Ascot? Why?

JULY

Wimbledon: this is one of the four great world tennis championships and the only one which is played on grass. It is held in the last week of June and the first week of July at Wimbledon in south-west London.

Henley Regatta: this is the largest rowing competition in Britain. It is held at Henley-on-Thames, where the Thames runs in a straight line for over two kilometres and makes it an ideal place for rowing. The regatta, or boat racing competition, has been held there almost every year since 1839.

Saint Swithin's Day: it is said that if it rains on Saint Swithin's Day, 15 July, it will rain for 40 days afterwards.

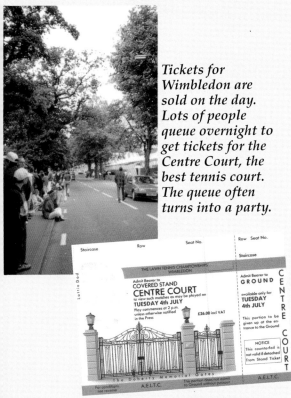

Tickets for Wimbledon are sold on the day. Lots of people queue overnight to get tickets for the Centre Court, the best tennis court. The queue often turns into a party.

3 a Is Wimbledon shown on TV in your country?
   b Describe how to get a ticket for the Centre Court at Wimbledon.

AUGUST

Thousands of people go to the Notting Hill Carnival for the party atmosphere!

Notting Hill Carnival: the last weekend in August there is a big carnival at Notting Hill in west London. People who take part dress up in fabulous costumes. Steel bands play African and Caribbean dance music and people dance and blow whistles. It's the biggest carnival outside Brazil.

The Proms: this is a popular series of classical music concerts. The season lasts seven weeks and there are concerts every night. Most of the concerts are performed at the Royal Albert Hall, in London. A lot of people like to go to the Last Night of the Proms. The orchestra plays popular tunes. People sing along and wave flags.

4 Make a calendar for an English-speaking friend to show what happens in your country in May, June, July and August. Explain what happens at each event and why.

The British year

SEPTEMBER

Blackpool Illuminations: every year 16 million visitors go to the holiday resort of Blackpool. When summer ends there are still things to see. From 1 September to 1 November, the promenade has a special illuminated display at night. The theme of the display changes every year.

Blackpool Illuminations along seven miles of promenades is the most visited attraction in Britain.

Harvest Festivals: in the autumn, harvest festivals are held. This is a Christian festival and churches are decorated with fruit, vegetables and flowers that people bring. Traditionally, the festival was held to say thank you to God for a good harvest.

People put their food and vegetables on the altar at the harvest festival.

1 What type of fruit and vegetables do you associate with a harvest festival?

OCTOBER

International Motor Show: every second year, car manufacturers from all over the world display their latest models at the National Exhibition Centre (NEC) in Birmingham.

Hallowe'en: 31 October is Hallowe'en. This pagan festival celebrates the return of the souls of the dead who come back to visit places where they used to live. In the evening there are lots of Hallowe'en parties, or fancy dress parties. People dress up as witches, ghosts, devils, cats, bats or anything scary. Houses are decorated with pumpkins with candles put inside. Some children follow the American custom called Trick or Treat. They knock at your house and ask, "Trick or treat?". If you give them some money or some sweets (a treat), they go away. Otherwise, they play a trick on you, like squirting water in your face.

HOW TO MAKE A HALLOWE'EN LANTERN

1. Cut two eyes, a nose and a mouth on one side of the hollowed pumpkin.

2. Cut the top and the bottom off the pumpkin. Keep the bottom piece for later.

3. Lower the 'head' over the candle, and light the candle.

4. Stand a candle in the piece cut off the bottom of the pumpkin.

5 Scoop the pulp from inside the pumpkin with a spoon.

2 The instructions for this Hallowe'en lantern are mixed up. Put them in the correct order.

NOVEMBER

London to Brighton Veteran Car Rally: this is usually the first Sunday in November. Hundreds of veteran cars are driven from London to Brighton, on the south coast of England.

The cars in the London to Brighton Veteran Car Rally were all built before 1905.

Guy Fawkes' Night (Bonfire Night): Guy Fawkes is Britain's most famous terrorist. On 5 November 1605, Guy Fawkes planned to blow up the Houses of Parliament and the King of England, James I. The plot was discovered and Guy Fawkes was hanged. Every year on 5 November, people celebrate by setting off fireworks. They also make models of Guy Fawkes and burn them on big bonfires.

3 Look at the Firework Code. Now close your books. Your partner wants to give a firework party. Give him/her some advice on handling fireworks.

DECEMBER

Pantomimes: these are plays put on before Christmas, usually for children. They are based on fairy tales, such as *Cinderella* or *Aladdin*, and mix comedy, song and dance.

Christmas cards: most people send Christmas cards to their friends and relations. Some shops sell charity cards and the profits made from selling these cards go to good causes.

Christmas Day: the most important day of the holidays is 25 December, or Christmas Day. Children wake up early to find a stocking full of small presents on their bed. Other presents, opened when everyone is together, are arranged around the Christmas tree, which is usually decorated with multicoloured lights. A traditional Christmas dinner includes roast turkey, roast potatoes and Brussels sprouts, followed by Christmas pudding.

Boxing Day: this is 26 December. It is usually spent in front of the TV recovering from Christmas Day.

A family enjoying a traditional Christmas dinner on 25 December.

4 **a** Design and make a Christmas card. Don't forget to write something inside.
   b Compare Christmas in Britain with Christmas in your country.
5 Which month of the year would you prefer to visit Britain? Why?

Many faiths

1 Match the religion to the festival.

a Christianity		**i**	Hanukka
b Hinduism		**ii**	Christmas
c Judaism		**iii**	Diwali
d Islam		**iv**	Eid ul-Fitr
e Sikhism		**v**	Guru Nanak's birthday

2 Read the text to find out if you are right.

A country of many religions 🎧

The official religion of Britain is Christianity. Schools in Britain must teach pupils about Christianity and Christian festivals, but Britain is a country in which many faiths are important.

Although 65 per cent of British people are Christian, very few of them go to church. More and more traditional churches are closing.

Other religions in Britain are Islam, Hinduism, Sikhism and Judaism. Altogether about 5 per cent of the population follow these faiths, and except for Judaism, they are all growing religions in Britain. There are 1.4 million Muslims, about 400,000 Hindus and about 600,000 Sikhs. Muslims, Sikhs and Hindus, in contrast to Christians, are more likely to practise their religion.

About 2 million Christians go to church on Sunday.

Festivals of light 🎧

Many religions celebrate major festivals with lights. Christians buy a tree at Christmas which they cover with lights.

Diwali, the five-day Hindu festival in late October, is often called the "Festival of Lights". The goddess Lakshmi comes at night to bless every house which is lit with candles. The candles are to welcome her.

Hanukka is an eight-day Jewish festival in December. Every night of this festival, a candle is lit in a special candlestick. People give presents and it is a time of great happiness.

Another time of great joy is the feast of Eid ul-Fitr. It is a Muslim feast which falls at different times every year. It marks the end of Ramadan, a fast during which Muslims do not eat or drink during the hours of daylight.

The great Sikh festival takes place in November and celebrates the birthday of their founder, the Guru Nanak, with processions, feasts and 24-hour readings of the Guru's writings.

Young girls light the last candle on the eighth day of Hanukka, the Jewish festival of lights.

The seasons 🎧

There are other festivals celebrated in Britain which are linked to the seasons. One of the most colourful and popular days in the Hindu year is Holi. This festival takes place in February or March and is the first day of spring in the Hindu calendar.

The Jews celebrate their New Year, Rosh Hashana, in September or October by sending cards.

The most spectacular New Year festival is the Chinese New Year. The Chinese New Year celebrations are enjoyed by many people, whether Chinese or not. In London's Chinatown, crowds watch processions, singing and dancing, kung fu displays and the Lion Dance. The lion walks down the street. In front of the lion, people bang on drums and crash cymbals. The lion stops in front of each Chinese shop and lifts its head up to get a string of green vegetables and some lucky money in a red envelope. The string is an offering to make sure that the dark days of winter go away and the light of the New Year comes back.

The Lion Dance is the most popular event of the Chinese New Year in Britain.

Festivals at school 🎧

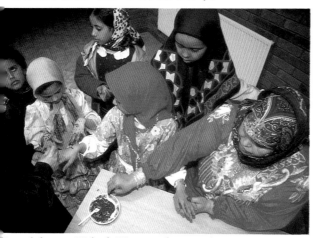

To celebrate Eid ul-Fitr mothers paint patterns on the feet and hands of the children.

Most religious festivals in Britain are not known or celebrated outside the relevant community, but many schools now try to celebrate the festivals of all the religions represented in Britain.

Take the Soho Parish School, a Church of England school in the heart of London: festivals of other major religions are given equal importance to Christmas. To celebrate Eid ul-Fitr, for example, Muslim mothers come into the school to cook traditional food and paint patterns on the children's hands.

You do not have to attend any religious festival, but normally everybody joins in. So, in the nativity play at Christmas, the Virgin Mary could be played by a Muslim girl and Joseph by a Buddhist Chinese boy.

3 Copy and complete the table using the information in the text, the pictures and your own general knowledge.

Name of the religion		Hinduism	Judaism		
Name of the person				Muslim	Sikh
Festivals	Christmas				
How festival is celebrated					

4 a Do you have an official religion in your country?
b Do you have to study Religion at school?
c Which religions exist in your country?
d Compare your country to Britain.

Coming to Britain

1 If you were going to Britain, how would you get there?

Travelling by boat

The English Channel has kept out invaders for a thousand years. Nowadays, Britain wants to welcome tourists, but the crossing makes travelling between Britain and the rest of Europe inconvenient and time-consuming. Despite that, about 18.1 million people visit Britain every year. Half of these people come to England by ferry or hovercraft.

The English Channel is one of the busiest stretches of water in the world and Dover, on the south coast of England, is the busiest passenger terminal in Europe. In August, the most popular month for visitors, there are 50 ferry and 14 hovercraft crossings between Dover and Calais every day. There are many routes across the Channel, but the fastest trip is the 35-minute hovercraft crossing between Dover and Calais.

Ferries take approximately 75 minutes for the crossing between Dover and Calais. Lots of people like taking the ferry. They often sit outside, if the weather is fine.

Three hours from Paris or Brussels to London

The ferry and hovercraft companies are worried about competition from the Channel Tunnel, or the "Chunnel" as it is commonly known.

The Chunnel was officially opened on 6 May 1994. It took ten years to build and cost £9.8 billion (more than double the original estimate). All of the money came from private companies.

There are two ways of travelling through the tunnel. Lorry and car drivers take their vehicles onto special trains. They stay inside their lorries and cars for the 20-minute journey through the tunnel. Foot passengers sit in a normal train compartment.

Direct trains already run from London to Paris and Brussels. The journey between London and the English coast is relatively slow in comparison to the journey between the French coast and Brussels and Paris. There have been considerable delays in planning the high-speed rail track in England and it is not due to open until 2002 at the earliest.

The entrance to the Channel Tunnel is near Folkestone. The train journey through the tunnel takes about 20 minutes.

Travelling by plane

London has five airports: Heathrow to the west, Gatwick to the south, Luton and Stansted to the north and the City Airport in the City of London. Heathrow Airport is the busiest international airport in the world, with 1,200 planes taking off and landing every day. Gatwick is the second busiest. Every year 94 million passengers use London's airports. The airports are vital, not only for the success of London's financial business in the City but also for tourism in Britain. London's links with the rest of the world are good, so many people change planes in London to catch long-distance flights.

People going to Britain do not always have to fly to London. Important cities with their own airports include Manchester, Glasgow, Birmingham, Edinburgh, Belfast, Aberdeen and Newcastle.

London City Airport has the shortest check-in time in Europe

Why waste time flying from anywhere else?

Frequent scheduled flights to

....ANTWERP · BRUSSELS · DUBLIN · FRANKFURT GENEVA · HAMBURG · HUMBERSIDE · LUGANO PARIS · ROTTERDAM · ZURICH....

London's first airport designed for the business traveller is attracting an increasing number of loyal, regular passengers, which should come as no surprise, considering what a civilised experience it makes of business flying.

No more than 15 minutes from the City (25 minutes from the West End), with no queues and a check-in time of only 10 minutes, London City Airport is the most time-saving, trouble free way to fly on business to more and more destinations within Europe.

LONDON CITY AIRPORT

Royal Docks, London E16 2PX.
Tel 0171-474 5555 Fax 0171 511 1040

Don't take a taxi from Heathrow, Gatwick or Stansted to the centre of London. The airports are a long way from the city centre and so taxi fares are very expensive! Public transport links are good from all of London's airports.

London City Airport is very near to the centre of London. It was built in the former London docks area.

2 Look at the advert for London City Airport. What type of people use London City Airport?

3 Choose a suitable way of arriving in Britain for the following people and give one reason for each choice.
  a A Swedish student.
  b A Parisian who needs to get to the centre of London in under 4 hours.
  c A Dutch or German couple who want to go on holiday to the south coast of England with their two children.
  d A Belgian businesswoman who has to be in the City of London for a meeting on Monday and in Zurich on Tuesday.
  e A man who wants to travel from Frankfurt to Manchester and who does not like confined spaces.

At home

1 **a** Describe the houses and flats in the photos.
b What type of families do you think live in them?

There's no place like home ∩

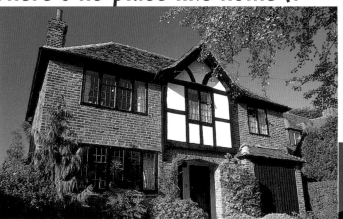

I live in a detached house about 15 miles outside Birmingham. It's a four-bedroomed house with a garden. We've got a snooker table in the games room downstairs. I like inviting my friends round to play.

I live with my Mum and my brothe in a semi-detached house. It's got three bedrooms. My brother has got the biggest bedroom. It' full of his stereo equipment. I have to knock before I can go in

About 80 per cent of British people live in houses. Detached houses are usually in expensive suburbs, quite far from the town centre, near to the countryside. Semi-detached houses are often in suburbs, which are nearer the town centre. Terraced houses and blocks of flats are mostly found in town centres. They can either be very small two-storey houses with one or two bedrooms or large houses with three to five floors and four or five bedrooms.

About 68 per cent of the people in Britain own their houses or flats. Most of the rest live in rented accommodation, including a small number in sheltered accommodation. People in Britain buy houses or flats because there is not enough accommodation for rent and it can be expensive.

I live with my boyfriend in a terraced house. It's quite small, bu I like living close to the town centre. We bought the house because it was cheaper to buy than to rent.

2 **a** Look at the photos. In which house or flat would you like to live?
b Describe your home.

Council housing ∩

Council flats and houses are built and owned by the local council. After the Second World War, a lot of high-rise council flats were constructed. Tower blocks could be 20 storeys high. Some blocks of flats were so badly built that they had to be pulled down only thirty years later.

Modern council housing estates are built differently now. There might be a mixture of two-storey terraced houses, together with a four-storey block of flats. There are play areas for children, and there is often a community centre, where people who live on the estate can meet.

Since the 1980s, council tenants have been able to buy their own homes very cheaply if they have lived in them for over two years. By 1993, 1.5 million council houses had been sold, but only a few thousand new council houses or flats are built every year. This means that it is now very difficult to find cheap housing for rent – a real problem for the poor and unemployed.

We've just moved into a two-bedroomed council house. I'm so pleased. I have been waiting for a council house for the last three years.

My family used to live here in a two-bedroomed council flat. It was terrible. The lifts were always breaking down, you didn't feel safe at night and there was absolutely nothing to do nearby.

In the garden ∩

Most British houses have a garden and many British people spend a lot of time in it. Most gardens, even small ones, have flowers and a lawn. If you don't have a garden, it is possible to grow flowers and vegetables on an allotment, which is a piece of land rented from the local council.

3 Copy and complete the sentences.
   a Most British people live in a ....
   b Most people in Britain .... their house or flat.
   c Most British homes have a ....
   d Detached houses are usually in the ....

4 Make a list of the differences in housing types between your country and Britain.

This is the back garden of a country cottage. Many British houses have front gardens too.

33

EVERY DAY In the family

1 What is your idea of a typical British family? Which of the following phrases describes your idea best?
 a Unmarried lone mother, with two children.
 b Young couple, living together, without children.
 c Elderly couple, married, whose children ha left home.
 d Divorced man, living alone.
 e Married couple, with child(ren) living at ho

2 Read the text to find out if you are right.

How big is your family?

We've been living together now for about two years. Neither of us really wants to get married, nor have children at the moment. Perhaps in a couple of years time.

NUMBER OF PEOPLE IN BRITISH HOUSEHOLDS

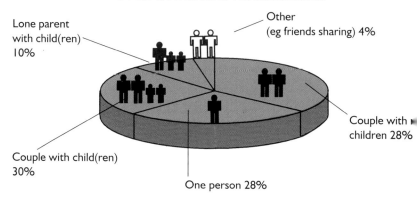

Lone parent with child(ren) 10%

Other (eg friends sharing) 4%

Couple with children 28%

Couple with child(ren) 30%

One person 28%

The most common type of household in England, Scotland and Wales today consists of a couple, either living together or married. About half of the couples have one or more children.

Twenty-eight per cent of households consist of people who live o their own. Most are widows, but there has been a big increase in the number of men who live alone. This is because so many couples ge divorced. Men often live on their own after getting divorced, whereas women often live with their children.

Nowadays, 10 per cent of families are lone parents with children. Women are usually the head of the household. Just over 20 per cent of families with children are headed by single mothers, with 2 per cent headed by a lone father.

This was the image of the traditional British household in the 1950s. Nowadays, only 7 per cent of British families consist of five or more people. The average British couple has 1.9 children.

3 Can you think of people you know who ...
 a have no children?
 b live on their own?
4 a Would you like to live on your own? Why (not)?
 b When do you think you will leave home?

34

Married life

Many couples live together before getting married and they call the person they live with a partner.
People still get married, but there is an increasing chance that the marriage will end in divorce. One in two marriages ends in divorce. The Government wants to help people to take more time to discuss their problems before they get divorced, so that they can perhaps sort things out and stay together. If people can talk about their problems, it may cause fewer problems for the children.

In Britain, you can get married in church or in a registry office.

Homelessness

Sometimes there can be 400 people sleeping on the streets of London every night. Thousands of others have no home, but sleep in hostels for the homeless. This accommodation is temporary, so they are always moving around. *The Big Issue* is a magazine, which talks about the problems of living on the streets. Some homeless people sell the magazine in the streets to earn money.
Finding somewhere cheap to live is not easy in Britain because there is not enough council housing or cheap rented accommodation. It is especially difficult for young people without work because they receive very little money from the state. If they are under 18, have left home and are not on a government work training scheme, they receive no money from the state.

5 If you could not live with your parents, what would you do?

*This **Big Issue** cover shows two homeless people who met and got married.*

Stay in or go out?

We asked some young people, "What do you like doing in the evening and at weekends?". Here are their answers.

Evening/weekend activities	Number of boys	Number of girls
Going out with friends	9	25
Visiting friends	3	3
Going shopping	8	9
Playing sport	16	9
Sleeping or relaxing	5	5
Reading books and magazines	5	10
Listening to music	4	5
Watching TV or videos	14	7
Playing computer games	5	0

6 Look at the table. True, false or don't know?
  a The boys seem to be more sociable than the girls.
  b Twice as many boys as girls watch TV or videos.
  c The most popular activity is visiting friends.
  d Young people prefer to go out rather than stay at home.
  e Some girls visit friends to listen to music.
7 Carry out a similar survey in your class.

Answers to 6 **a** false; **b** true; **c** false; **d** true; **e** don't know.

EDUCATION *At school*

1 Answer these questions for your country.
 a At what age do you have to start school?
 b At what age can you leave school?
 c At what age do you normally take exams or tests?

Secondary school

Most secondary schools in Britain are comprehensive schools. These are state schools, which take children of all abilities. About six per cent of students go to grammar schools, state schools which only take students who pass an examination at the age of 11.

About seven per cent of students go to private schools. These schools do not receive any money from the state: parents pay for their children to go to school instead. Most expensive private schools are called public schools. Most of these are single-sex boarding schools, where students live during term-time.

Most pupils in British schools wear school uniform. The favourite colours for school uniforms are blue, grey, black and maroon.

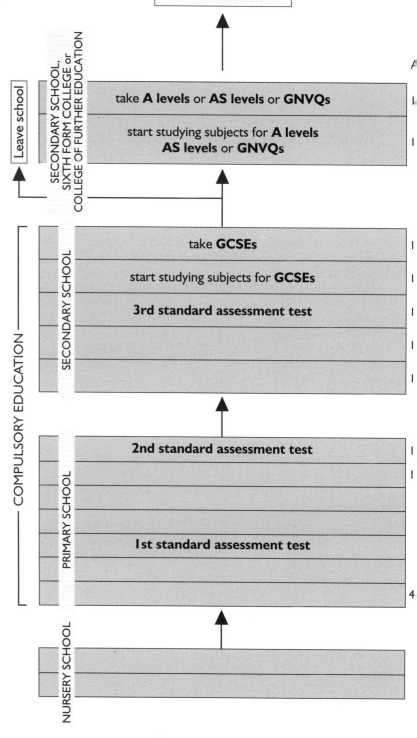

Go to work or COLLEGE of HIGHER EDUCATION or UNIVERSITY

Leave school

SECONDARY SCHOOL, SIXTH FORM COLLEGE or COLLEGE OF FURTHER EDUCATION

take **A levels** or **AS levels** or **GNVQs**

start studying subjects for **A levels AS levels** or **GNVQs**

COMPULSORY EDUCATION

SECONDARY SCHOOL

take **GCSEs**

start studying subjects for **GCSEs**

3rd standard assessment test

PRIMARY SCHOOL

2nd standard assessment test

1st standard assessment test

NURSERY SCHOOL

The National Curriculum

In 1988, for the first time in British history, a National Curriculum was introduced. The National Curriculum tells pupils which subjects they have to study, what they must learn and when they have to take assessment tests.

Between the ages of 14 and 16, pupils study for their GCSE (General Certificate of Secondary Education) exams. Pupils must take English Language, Maths and Science for GCSE, as well as a half GCSE in a foreign language and Technology. In addition, they must also be taught Physical Education, Religious Education and Sex Education, although they do not take exams in these subjects.

At the age of 16, pupils can leave school. If pupils stay on, they usually take A (Advanced) levels, AS (Advanced Supplementary) level or GNVQs (Greater National Vocational Qualifications). It is quite common to combine, for example, two A levels with one AS level, or one A level with one GNVQ.

Pupils taking A levels study traditional subjects, such as French, Physics or History. To go to university, pupils usually need two or three A levels.

AS levels are the same standard as A levels, but

Fifth-form pupils in their I.T. (computer) class at Chancellors School in Norwich.

only half the content: AS level German pupils take the A-level German language exam, but do not take the A-level German Literature exam.

GNVQs are vocational qualifications. Pupils usually take on GNVQ in subjects such as Business, Leisure and Tourism, Manufacturing, and Art and Design. One GVNQ (at advanced level) is equal to two A levels.

2 | Read the text and look at the diagram. Now answer Exercise one for Britain. Compare Britain to your country.

The school day

Hello! I'm Steve. I'm fifteen and I'm in the fifth form at St Mary's Comprehensive School. This is my timetable. I play for the school football team so during lunch or after school, I have football training.

3 | a What time does school start and finish?
b How many foreign languages is Steve studying?
c How much time does he spend doing sport?
d How does this compare with your timetable?

Time	Monday	Tuesday	Wednesday	Thursday	Friday
8.30 - 8.40	registration	registration	registration	registration	registration
8.40 - 9.00	assembly	assembly	assembly	assembly	assembly
9.00 - 9.45	French	Technology	S.E.	Art	R.E.
9.45 - 10.30	French	Science	Maths	Art	I.T.
10.30- 11.15	Science	Science	Maths	French	Science
11.15- 11.30	break	break	break	break	break
11.30- 12.15	Maths	History	English Literature	Science	Technology
12.15- 1.00	Maths	History	English Literature	Science	Technology
1.00 - 2.00	lunch	lunch	lunch	lunch	lunch
2.00 - 2.45	English Language	Art	P.E.	History	English Language
2.45 - 3.30	English Language	Art	P.E.	English Language	English Language

P.E. = Physical Education; I.T. = Information Technology; S.E. = Sex Education R.E. = Religious Education

EDUCATION At college

1 **a** List the different things you can do in your country when you leave school.
b Read the text and list the different things you can do in Britain when you leave school.

Universities and colleges

Most big towns in Britain have both a university and a college of higher education. There are 91 universities in Britain and 47 colleges of higher education. Universities offer three- and four-year degree courses; colleges of higher education offer both two-year HND (Higher National Diploma) courses, as well as degree courses.

A degree is a qualification you get from university when you pass your final exams. You are then awarded a BA (Bachelor of Arts), BSc (Bachelor of Science) or BEd (Bachelor of Education).

Undergraduates – students who are studying for degrees – go to large, formal lectures, but most of the work takes place in tutorials: lessons in groups of ten or more when the students discuss their work with the lecturer.

A tutorial at Birmingham University.

Kathryn, a Law graduate, has just received her degree.

Getting into university

Only 25 per cent of the student population go on to higher education. Competition to get into one of Britain's universities is fierce and not everyone who gets A levels can go. Students usually need three A levels to go to university and grades at A level go from A, the highest grade, down to E.

Students apply to universities months before they take their A levels. The students are given a personal interview and the universities decide which students they want. The place which a student is offered depends on his or her A-level results. The more popular a university, the higher the grades it will ask for. If students do not get the grades that a university asks for, they have to try to get a place at another university or college before the new term starts in early October.

> My name is Miriam. I've just got my A-level results and I'm really worried. Nottingham University said they would only accept me if I got two Bs and a C, but I only got one B and two Cs!

Living at university

Most British students choose to go to university a long way from their home town. They think going to university is a time to be independent, and to live away from home and develop new interests.

Until 1998, British students did not have to pay to go to university. Now they must pay about £1,000 a year as a tuition fee. They also need money to live away from home. Many students, whose parents do not earn a lot of money, are given a grant from the local education authority. If students do not get a grant, parents are expected to pay for their children. Some students borrow money from the bank, which must be paid back after they leave university. In theory, the grant pays for rent, food, books and transport. In fact, the grant is not large enough. Students often work during the holidays to earn more money. About 38 per cent of the population under 24 years of age go on to higher education.

OXFORD AND CAMBRIDGE

Oxford and Cambridge are the oldest universities in Britain and they have the highest academic reputation. This photo is of Oxford. Most of the colleges are built around courtyards, called quads, with lawns in the centre.

Training

Many companies run their own in-house training schemes. These trainees are learning about retailing.

Not all students study full-time at university or college. Many people combine their studies with work. Some companies release their staff for training one or two days a week or for two months a year. Large companies often have their own in-house training schemes.

The British Government is very enthusiastic about such training schemes. It wants at least half the work force to have a formal professional qualification by the year 2000. The Government introduced a New Deal scheme in 1998, which aims to help people who are unemployed find jobs or train for the work they want to do.

2   **a** Give one advantage of going to university or college in Britain.
   b Give one advantage of training schemes in Britain.
   c Can students in Britain choose which university they go to?

   d If you got good grades at A level, but you did not get a grant and your parents refused to give you any money, what would you do?
   e If you did not get good grades at A level, what would you do?

1 a At what age can you get a part-time job in your country?
b Have your parents ever been unemployed?

Part-time work 🎧

Women with children often take part-time jobs. Some mothers want to work full-time, but cannot because it is difficult for them to find someone to look after their children. In Britain, there are very few nurseries for young children.

Partners often have to look after the children while women work part-time in the early morning or in the evening. It is more difficult for single mothers to take on part-time work because they must earn enough to pay someone to look after their children.

In April 1999, the Government introduced a minimum wage per hour for workers, but it is not very much. People over 22 are paid £3.60 per hour and younger workers between 18 and 21 receive £3.00. Part-time workers now also have more rights including holiday pay.

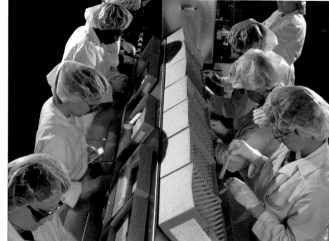

There are more part-time jobs in Britain than in any other European country. Eighty per cent of part-time jobs are done by women.

2 Do a survey in your class.
a How many people have mothers who work?
b Do they work part-time or full-time?
c Compare your country with Britain.

No qualifications, no job 🎧

There are fewer jobs for unskilled people in Britain than before. Only about two-thirds of men without qualifications have jobs. Some of the unskilled jobs available are working in restaurants, in supermarkets filling shelves or as a checkout operator, or cleaning. If there is any unskilled work, it is offered to women because, despite laws for equal pay, women are still paid less than men. Even job seekers with qualifications sometimes find it difficult to find permanent, full-time work.

Martin, from Sheffield, has a degree in history. He works part-time as a waiter in the evenings and temps as a bike courier when there is work.

3 a What job would you like to do when you leave school?
b What qualifications do you need to do the job?

Without work and poor

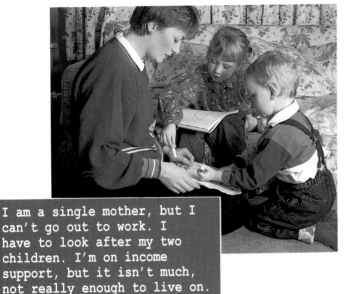

I am a single mother, but I can't go out to work. I have to look after my two children. I'm on income support, but it isn't much, not really enough to live on.

People in Britain who are unemployed sign on every two weeks and claim their unemployment benefit. When people say that they are "on the dole", it means that they are receiving unemployment benefit.

Some people cannot claim this money, even though they do not go out to work. Single parents, for example, do not receive unemployment benefit, they have income support. People who are on income support receive less money than those on unemployment benefit.

Nearly seven million people are now living on income support. Many experts know that people on unemployment benefit or income support do not have enough money to live on.

QUIZ

We asked boys and girls aged 15 and 16 what they thought they would be doing in ten years' time. Guess the results. When you have guessed, look at the answers below.

What about the future?

1 The percentage of girls who thought they would be married and not at work was:
a None
b 8%
c 30%
d 62%

2 The percentage of girls and boys who wanted to be teachers was:
a None
b 14%
c 27%
d 59%

3 The most popular job for boys was:
a sportsman
b engineer
c computer programmer
d journalist

4 Jobs chosen by both girls and boys were:
a chef
b banker
c electrician
d fire-fighter

5 Jobs chosen only by boys were:
a journalist
b D.J.
c computer engineer
d car salesperson

6 Jobs chosen only by girls were:
a dancer
b D.J.
c cartoonist
d doctor

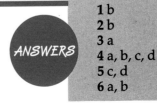

ANSWERS

1 b
2 b
3 a
4 a, b, c, d
5 c, d
6 a, b

4 **a** The survey shows that girls are (not) interested in ....
   b The survey shows that boys are (not) interested in ....
5 Now carry out a similar survey in your own class or school. Make a list of the questions you want to ask. Write the questionnaire and give it to all your friends (at least ten people). Compare your results with the British survey.

WORKING LIFE — The economy

1 Do you think the following people work in a service industry or a manufacturing industry?

a research chemist for a drugs company   **d** bank cashier
b aircraft factory worker   **e** travel agent
c insurance salesperson   **f** sales assistant

2 Read the text to find out if you are right.

British industry

Britain used to have many manufacturing industries, but since the Second World War it is service industries, especially banking and retailing, which have expanded. About 70 per cent of people now work in service industries, including tourism, insurance, computer technology and retailing. Less than 30 per cent of people have jobs in industry.

Heavy industries like steel manufacture and shipbuilding have been replaced by high-technology manufacturing industries such as aeroplane engines and pharmaceuticals.

Two and a half million people work in retailing (shops, supermarkets, chain-stores) in Britain. It is one of Britain's biggest service industries.

The City

LIFFE (a futures market for financial products and commodities like sugar and cocoa) started in 1992. It is now the second-largest market of its kind in the world.

The City is a part of London. It used to be the old Roman and medieval town of London, but is now the area of London with all the banks. The City is one of the most important financial centres in the world. Although the City is only one square mile (2.5 km^2), 300,000 people work there. It contains 555 banks from many different countries.

The City earns over £25 billion a year by selling its financial services. Every year it handles 32 per cent of the world's foreign exchange trade (buying and selling of foreign currencies), twice as much as the next main centre, New York.

Made in Britain

In Britain, there are only a few successful large companies, but many successful small companies. The large companies often invest a lot of money in research and development, R & D, to find new and better, usually high-technology, products.

Successful small manufacturing companies in Britain often make expensive products. These companies are successful because they use first-class materials, have excellent quality control and the workers are proud of what they make. They include J. Barbour & Sons, which makes waterproof jackets; Morgan Motor Company, which makes élite cars; Quad Electroacoustics, which makes top-quality hi-fi equipment; Wilkin & Sons, which makes jams.

Barbour jackets, originally ▲ designed for fishermen and farmers, are now fashionable in cities throughout Europe.

Glaxo Wellcome is Britain's leading pharmaceutical company and is one of the largest in the world. It tries to find and make new medicines which can cure or reduce the effects of disease. ▼

BP Amoco is now the ▶ *second-largest oil company in the world. It is involved in oil and gas exploration, oil refining and the manufacture of petrochemical products. It is investing money in making cleaner petrol.*

ENTREPRENEURS

Richard Branson is Britain's most famous entrepreneur. The Virgin companies include record shops, an airline, a train service, a radio station and a clothes company.

Quad ▶ *Electroacoustics is well-known for its expensive but high-quality loudspeakers and hi-fi equipment.*

3 True or false?
  a There are more people working in manufacturing industries than in service industries in Britain.
  b The City is a powerful financial centre.
  c BP Amoco is a service industry.
  d Glaxo Wellcome is a service industry.
  e Richard Branson is a successful businessman.
4 Name two successful companies from your country.

43

FOOD

1 Look at the photos.
  a Which meal do you think is most "British"?
  b Which meal would you like to eat most? Least?
2 a How often do you sit down at table to eat with your
  parents?

Traditional British

Hotels often serve afternoon tea.

Britain has some excellent traditional
food: lamb from Wales, shellfish and
fresh salmon from Northern Ireland,
fresh or smoked fish from Scotland,
cheeses from England and Wales.

Unfortunately, good British food
can be difficult to find. Only a few
restaurants in London serve British
food. There are many more Italian,
Chinese and Indian restaurants.

A British fried breakfast.

British food tends to be either very expensive and
found in luxury hotels or restaurants, or mainly fried
food served in cheaper cafés. Most pubs now serve
good value hot and cold meals. They often have
family areas where people under 16 can sit and eat.

East meets West

Most British people, if they go out for a meal or
buy a takeaway, go to their local Indian or Chinese
restaurant. There are 8,000 Indian restaurants in
Great Britain and most towns, however small,
have one.

Indian restaurants serve food from India,
Pakistan and Bangladesh. North Indian food is the
most common: spicy curries of meat or vegetables
are served with rice or different types of bread.
South Indian food is often vegetarian since most
southern Indians are Hindu and eat little or no
meat.

Most Chinese restaurants serve Cantonese food,
including lunch-time snacks called dim sum:
steamed or deep-fried dumplings, with either
savoury or sweet fillings.

Chinese and Indian restaurants in Britain now
face competition from Thai restaurants. Thai
cuisine is often very spicy and uses some of the
same ingredients as Chinese food.

*Indian dishes are spicy and can be either mild or
hot. The hot dishes are very, very hot!*

Fast food 🎧

People in Britain are more likely to eat fast food than to go out to eat in a posh restaurant. A hamburger and French fries is the most popular fast-food meal in Britain, but not all fast food is American. Kebab houses, often run by Greek or Turkish Cypriots, are also very popular. Customers choose from chicken or lamb kebabs, served with salad in bread. People also like to eat baked potatoes filled with cheese and other fillings and pizza with lots of different toppings.

People spend less time cooking now. An increasing number of people eat convenience food in the evenings. Convenience meals are already cooked – all you have to do is heat them up in the microwave or the oven.

The traditional, British fast-food meal is fish and chips.

A hamburger, French fries and a milkshake from an American chain of fast-food restaurants.

For my dinner, I eat pot noodles, which I heat up in the microwave, and maybe a packet of crisps. I'll have some chocolate and probably a yogurt. If there's Coke in the house, then I drink that. Otherwise, I have a glass of orange juice. I like to eat my dinner in my room, watching TV.

VEGETARIAN FOOD

About seven per cent of British people are vegetarian. If you are vegetarian, eating out is quite easy in Britain because there are vegetarian restaurants. Vegetarians and many other people are worried about genetically modified food and the effect it can have on the environment. They try to eat organically grown food.

3 Do you think convenience food is fast food?

4 a Which of the dishes mentioned in the text can you find in your country?

b How different is British food from the food in your country?

c Do you think eating habits in your country are healthy?

Film and theatre

1 **a** How often do you go to the cinema or the theatre?
b What is your favourite film or play this year? Is it British?

> I love going to the cinema. I go about twice a month. I even love the trailers!

Going to the cinema

Going to the cinema is very popular in Britain, especially with young people, between 15 and 24. They often like to buy popcorn to eat or drink milkshakes while they watch a film.

Many multiplexes, cinema complexes with up to 14 screens showing a wide range of films, have been built. These multiplexes have encouraged more people to go to the cinema.

British men and women have different tastes in films. In a survey, most men liked action films which they watched on television or on video. Women preferred films which dealt with human relations between friends or between men and women.

2 Carry out a similar survey in your school. Decide what questions to ask and write the questionnaire. Ask a friend to fill in the questionnaire. Make a bar chart of the results in your class and compare your results with the British survey.

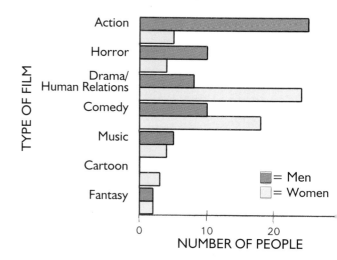

The British film industry

Four Weddings and a Funeral *is one of the most popular British films ever made.*

Most of the films that people go to see at the cinema in Britain are made in Hollywood. The British film industry does exist, but it is very small. The films do not have big budgets, so they cannot compete easily with American films. British people who want to make films often go to America. Hollywood is full of British actors, directors, writers, editors and camera people.

A few films made by British film companies receive some money from American companies. This means that British films often have to use American actors to appeal to an American cinema-going audience. Some films made in Britain, like *Four Weddings and a Funeral*, *Trainspotting*, *The Full Monty* and *Notting Hill*, have been very successful around the world.

he theatre

Sir Anthony Hopkins and Emma Thompson are famous British actors.

The audience enjoying a play at a commercial theatre in London.

Britain has a long tradition of drama. British theatre began in the thirteenth century, before the time of Shakespeare, with a series of short stories from the Bible called *the Mystery Plays*. Ordinary people still perform these plays every four years in York and Chester.

Acting, both by amateurs and professionals, is still very much alive in Britain. British professional actors are usually highly respected and well-trained. Some actors start their careers in the British theatre and then go to work in British and American films.

The most famous British theatres are the National Theatre and the Barbican. The Royal Shakespeare Company performs at the Barbican in London and in Stratford-on-Avon, where Shakespeare was born. In spite of the money, many theatres receive from the government, they find it difficult to survive.

There are many smaller theatre groups in Britain. Some of them receive government money to perform plays which are contemporary and experimental. Commercial theatres do not receive any money from the Government. They usually perform very popular plays. If a play is successful, the company will perform it for many years.

heatre in London

Most British cities have a theatre, but London has the greatest number. There are over 50 theatres in London's West End, the area in London with most theatres, and about 35 smaller fringe theatres.

In recent years, musicals have been very successful. About 5½ million people, many of them tourists, go to see a musical every year in London.

Going to the theatre in Britain is not only popular, but also expensive. Not many young people can afford to go. It is possible to get cheaper tickets by going to afternoon performances called matinees or by buying stand-bys, half-price tickets which are sold half an hour before a performance starts.

3 Give two differences between going to the theatre and going to the cinema.

*The best-known contemporary composer of musicals is Andrew Lloyd Webber. At the moment there are four of his productions in London. **Cats** is his longest-running musical.*

47

THE ARTS Music

1 We asked 60 British teenagers, "What is your favourite type of music?". On the right are some of their answers. Which types of music do you know? Which types of music do you like?

- heavy metal
- house
- indie
- pop
- ragga
- rap
- soul
- rave
- techno
- reggae

Music, music, music

Rave night at the local club.

The British music scene is extremely varied. There are many different types of music and groups that you can enjoy. If you want to, you can go to a techno night at the local club on Friday, a classical concert on Saturday and see a reggae band live on stage on Sunday.

It is difficult for groups in Britain to have lots of fans or sell lots of records because there are so many different types of music. There are even more types than are listed above. Bands do not last long and very few groups stay in the Top 20, a list of the best-selling records, for more than one or two weeks. Even if they are in the Top 20, it does not necessarily mean that they sell many records.

2 Read the text again. What do the following phrases mean in your language?

a a band
b live on stage
c a techno night
d the local club
e lots of fans
g The Top 20

3 Think about a music style in your country. Describe the clothes that the fans wear.

International influences

Pop music in Britain is influenced by music from all over the world. Many teenagers in our survey liked reggae, which comes from Jamaica. Boys also enjoyed dancing and listening to Black-American rap.

Some music in Britain is a mixture of styles. Ragga brings together rap and reggae, for example. Pop music is also influencing traditional music. Recently some young musicians of Asian origin have started to mix bhangra (traditional music from the Punjab region) with Western pop.

4 Copy and complete this questionnaire. Then ask your partner for his/her views.

	Me	My partner
Favourite group		
Favourite singer		
Favourite single		
Favourite CD		
Favourite concert		
Favourite video		
Favourite type of music		

Clubs

Most clubs play different types of music and attract different types of clubbers each night. For example, Fridays might be "rave nights" when the DJ plays only rave music. To get into many clubs you have to be over 18 or 21. Sometimes you have to be a member and there's often a dress code: if they don't like the way you look, they will not let you in. Often you just have to look trendy.

An invitation to a jungle night.

An invitation to a techno night.

Flyers are given to people waiting to go into clubs or when they leave clubs. They are invitations to future musical events. Each kind of music has its own style of flyer.

An invitation to a soul night.

5 **a** Which invitation do you like most? Why?
b Design your own invitation. Think about the music style of your club. Make sure the invitation tells you what type of music night it is. Don't forget the date, the address, how much it costs or the name of the DJ.

THE ARTS *The classics*

1 Match the books with their authors.
  a Jane Austen   **i** *Far from the Madding Crowd*
  b Emily Brontë   **ii** *Oliver Twist*
  c Charles Dickens   **iii** *Pride and Prejudice*
  d Thomas Hardy   **iv** *Wuthering Heights*

2 Read the text to find out if you are right.

William Shakespeare ♫

William Shakespeare, Britain's greatest playwright, was born in Stratford-on-Avon in England. Stratford is now the second most-visited town in Britain. People come to see his plays, performed by the Royal Shakespeare Company at the theatre which is named after him, and to see his tomb.

In the early 1590s, Shakespeare went to London. He set up his own theatre, the Globe, where his company performed his plays. An exact reconstruction of the Globe has been built and visitors can now experience what it was like to go to the theatre 400 years ago. Plays can be seen there from May to September, though the theatre is open to the public all year round.

During Shakespeare's lifetime, most of his plays were performed at the Globe Theatre in London.

Charles Dickens ♫

Oliver Twist is the story of an orphan thrown out of the poor house because he asks for more food.

Dickens was probably the most popular novelist in the English language in the nineteenth century. When he was only 12, Charles had to leave school and work in a factory. His novels often tell the stories of young children who work hard to escape a life of poverty. Many of the stories were set in London and his novels show how the city changed during his lifetime.

Most of his books first appeared as serials in magazines. Each week or month, Dickens had to write another chapter of his story. He had to write fast and sometimes changed the stories if the public did not like his last chapter or particularly liked certain characters.

3 **a** With what parts of Britain is each novelist linked? Why?
    b Make a list of four of your country's most famous novelists. Do they write about the country or the city? Imaginary towns or real towns? Rich people or poor people?

Charlotte, Emily and Anne Brontë 🎧

The Brontë sisters were exceptional writers of poetry as well as fiction. Between 1847 and 1848, all three sisters published novels. They wrote under pen names, because books written by women were not always accepted as easily as books written by men. Emily Brontë became Ellis Bell; Charlotte Brontë was Currer Bell and Anne Brontë, Acton Bell.

Wuthering Heights by Emily Brontë is the most famous of the Brontë novels. The story tells of the destructive and passionate love between Catherine and Heathcliff, who grow up together on a farm called Wuthering Heights. Heathcliff leaves the farm when Catherine, for reasons of social class, refuses to marry him.

All three sisters died very young. They all lived in Yorkshire where the novel *Wuthering Heights* is set.

Catherine and Heathcliff both loved and hated each other.

Thomas Hardy 🎧

Thomas Hardy was a poet and a novelist. He wrote about the English countryside, in particular Dorset in south-west England, where he came from. His books include romantic love stories and show how farming life was changing quickly with the introduction of machines. The stories are set in Wessex, an ancient name for a region in south-west England. The places are based on real towns and villages. In the book *Far from the Madding Crowd*, the town of Casterbridge is the real town of Dorchester.

The last two Hardy novels, *Tess of the D'Urbervilles* and *Jude the Obscure*, were both very controversial, particularly because of their treatment of sexual passion. Annoyed at the public reaction, Hardy spent the rest of his life writing poetry.

This photo shows the market in Casterbridge, in a TV version of **Far from the Madding Crowd.**

Jane Austen 🎧

Jane Austen spent her short life in Hampshire, near the south coast of England. Her novels describe the everyday life of people in the upper-middle class circles she knew best. Money and social position were very important and the only role of a woman of that class was to find a rich husband.

Her characters spend most of the time in the countryside, doing little or no work. Occasionally they go to London; sometimes they go to Bath, a fashionable town. Her novels may sound boring, but they are a record of what life was like for the upper-middle class in the early nineteenth century and are among the finest and most entertaining novels written at the time.

These stamps show scenes from Jane Austen's novels: they show what life was like for the upper class in early nineteenth-century England.

THE ARTS Modern life

1 **a** How often do you read modern novels?
b How often do you read poetry?
c What modern literature do you read at school?

Women writers

There have always been good women writers, but until the 1950s it was not easy for a woman writer to sell many of her books under her own name. Many nineteenth-century women writers used male pen names or pseudonyms: George Eliot, an important nineteenth-century writer (1819–1880), never used her real name which was Mary Ann Evans.

Things are changing. Since the 1950s, the number of well-known women writers has increased. Women writers are now winning prizes for literature. Nadine Gordimer, a South African writer, won the Nobel Prize for Literature in 1991 with *July's People*.

Jeanette Winterson's **Oranges Are Not The Only Fruit** *(1985) was a very popular novel. It tells the story of a young girl who rebels against her strict family life. The book was made into a television series.*

Multicultural English literature

A number of writers have used life in the former British colonies as the background for their novels. Some British novelists of Indian or Carribean ethnic origin write about how they see the two different cultures.

English literature has also benefited from the work of Indian, African and Asian authors who write in English and who write novels from the point of view of the colonised, rather than the colonisers. Chinua Achebe, a Nigerian author, wrote *Things Fall Apart* (1958). The story tells how an important man in the Obi tribe is forced, by his own people, to leave his village because he does not want white, English missionaries to come. Arundhati Roy is an Indian writer, who wrote a well-known book *The God of Small Things* (1997), which is set in India.

The Buddha of Suburbia *by Hanif Kureishi (1990) is the story of a young British boy, with an Indian father and a British mother, growing up in a London suburb.*

OTHER MODERN WRITERS TO TRY		
A.S. Byatt	Doris Lessing	Timothy Mo
Anita Brookner	Penelope Lively	R.K. Narayan

Poetry and speech

Some writers are changing the way English is written. They write English to show the way that they speak the language. They try to show rhythm and local accent in their work. This started in the 1960s with a group of poets from the city of Liverpool. Their poems are best understood when they are read aloud. Bookshops now arrange performances of modern poets' work and this has helped to make poetry more popular.

Benjamin Zephaniah, a British writer from the Caribbean, uses rap rhythms to write poetry. He says he started writing his own poetry because he didn't like the poetry he had to read at school.

STRANGE STORIES

*Some modern authors write stories about strange animals, violent human beings and bizarre events. One of the best writers of such stories was Angela Carter (1940–1992). In **The Magic Toyshop** (1967), the reader is never sure if Melanie, the teenage heroine, is going mad, dreaming or under the spell of her uncle's magic puppets. The book was made into a film.*

Rapid rapping (rant) by Benjamin Zephaniah

Intellectuals and sociologists mus come an see
What is happening now orally,
It is really meking history bringing poetry alive
To a dub or funky reggae, to jazz music, rock an jive,
Yu cannot ignore it as de people voice dere feelings
Some are sick of politricks an diplomatic double dealing
So dey picking up de microphone fe dere expression
Dey hav fe get it right or dey get verbal reaction.

2 Look at the extract from *Rapid Rapping* by Benjamin Zephaniah. What is the usual spelling of the following words?
  a mus   f dere
  b an   g dey
  c meking   h fe
  d Yu   i hav fe
  e de
3 Read the poem aloud.
4 What do you think about what Benjamin Zephaniah says about poetry (see caption)? Do you agree or not?
5 You can read all the novels mentioned in the text. They have all won prizes or been made into films. Which one would you like to read?
6 Describe a modern novel which you have read. Include the following information:
  • the author
  • the name of the main character(s)
  • the story
  • four adjectives to describe the novel

THE MEDIA In the news

1 Do you think the following sentences are true or false?
   a British people read a lot of newspapers.
   b Broadsheets are more popular than tabloids.
   c British children prefer magazines to newspapers.
   d More boys than girls in Britain buy magazines.
2 Read the text to find out if you are right.

The national press

British people like reading newspapers. More newspapers are read in Britain than in any other European country.

There are two types of newspaper in Britain: tabloid and broadsheet. The two most popular daily newspapers, *The Sun* and *The Daily Mirror,* are both tabloids. Tabloids have lots of stories about famous people; the photos are large; the headlines are big and there is not much text. Tabloids sell many more copies than broadsheets.

Broadsheets, such as *The Times,* are not as popular as the tabloids. Broadsheets have long articles with lots of information; some pages report international news; the photos and the headlines are smaller than in the tabloids.

The differences between the tabloids and the broadsheets are breaking down. Broadsheets now realise that tabloids are easier to read and hold. *The Guardian,* a broadsheet, now has a tabloid section. Many of the broadsheets now have stories about famous people. Tabloids used to be cheaper than broadsheets, but *The Times* is now the cheapest national newspaper.

A broadsheet newspaper is double the size of a tabloid newspaper. A broadsheet is more difficult to hold when you are reading it.

Sunday newspapers are a part of the British way of life. These newspapers only appear on Sundays and are more popular than the daily newspapers. They concentrate on general issues and famous people. Some people spend all day reading the Sunday newspaper.

Paperboys and papergirls deliver the newspaper to over 60 per cent of British families every morning. Boys and girls who earn money delivering newspapers must get permission from their parents and headteacher.

3 List all the newspapers you know. Are they tabloid or broadsheet?

Magazines

There are thousands of weekly and monthly magazines in Britain. These can be divided into four main categories: specialist magazines, such as the computer magazine *PC Weekly*; general magazines, such as the TV listings magazine *Radio Times*; women's magazines and teenage magazines.

Young people below the age of 18 do not buy newspapers, but they do buy magazines. The favourite magazines of 15-year-olds are shown in the chart. Many more girls than boys buy magazines. Their main interests seem to be boys, pop music, clothes and make-up. Teenage girls like reading magazines which are aimed at an older age group. *Sugar* is not only the most popular magazine for 15-year-olds, it is also very popular with 12-year-olds.

> I wish there were more magazines for boys. If you don't like football magazines or computer-games magazines, there is nothing for you to read.

FAVOURITE MAGAZINES OF 15-YEAR-OLDS

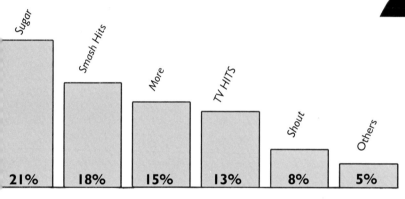

Sugar	Smash Hits	More	TV HITS	Shout	Others
21%	18%	15%	13%	8%	5%

Smash Hits is a music magazine which both girls and boys buy.

Shout is popular with young teenage girls.

TV Hits is about TV stars, film stars and pop stars.

Sugar is one of the most popular girl's magazines.

4   a Look at the covers of the magazines. Using the text, the covers and the chart describe the people who read the magazines.
   b Describe magazines that you know which are similar to *Sugar*, *Smash Hits*, *TV Hits* and *Shout*.
   c Do a survey. Which magazines are the most popular in your class? Is there any difference between what boys read and girls read?

THE MEDIA — On TV and radio

1 a When do you watch TV?
b When do you listen to the radio?

> I'd like to get satellite TV —
> it has a channel devoted to
> sport and also the music
> channel, MTV — but my parents
> say the subscription is too
> expensive.

What's on "the box"? 🎧

Over 99 per cent of British homes have a TV and the average person watches "the box" 24 hours a week. There are five (non-satellite) TV channels in Britain: BBC1, BBC2, ITV, Channel 4 and Channel 5. BBC1 and BBC2, the two state channels, do not show adverts. ITV, Channel 4 and Channel 5, the three independent channels, do show adverts.

BBC1 and ITV tend to broadcast popular programmes: sports programmes, recent films, news, game shows, children's programmes and soaps. BBC2 and Channel 4 show programmes which usually attract much smaller audiences: TV plays, classical concerts, foreign films and programmes for minority groups. Channel 5 offers mainly game shows and second rate American films. About 26 per cent of British homes subscribe to satellite or cable TV.

*The wildlife documentary series, **Life in the Freezer**, introduced by David Attenborough, was particularly popular.*

Battle of the soaps 🎧

Soaps are popular TV serials which dramatise their characters' daily lives. The storylines are entertaining, but often unbelievable. Soaps are broadcast either three or five times a week and each episode lasts about half an hour. Nearly half the population watches one or both of the two most popular soaps, *Coronation Street* and *Eastenders*.

Coronation Street has been running since December 1960 and is set in a working-class area of Manchester. *Eastenders* is set in the East End of London. Since 1985, when it was first broadcast, it has introduced controversial issues, such as racial prejudice and AIDS.

The two Australian soaps, *Neighbours* and *Home and Away*, are shown five days a week and children watch them when they come in from school. They are the favourite programmes of both 12- and 15-year-olds.

*Each episode of **Coronation Street** is watched by up to 17 million people. It is so popular that people visit television studios in Manchester to look round the set.*

2 a Compare your TV watching habits with the average person in Britain.
b Do you have satellite or cable TV? Compare your country with Britain.
c What is the most popular programme on TV in your country? Is it a soap?
d Does your country show British TV programmes? Are they dubbed or sub-titled?

et's watch a video 🎧

About 79 per cent of UK households now have a video recorder. People mostly use them to record TV programmes which they watch at a more convenient time. At weekends, people also go to a video shop to rent a film instead of going to the cinema. Teenagers aged between 14 and 16 like getting together with friends to watch a video. They often choose films with an 18 rating. These videos are unsuitable for people below the age of 18 because they are violent, but many teenagers watch them anyway.

Lots of children try to rent videos with an 18 rating, especially the really violent movies. By law, I'm not allowed to rent videos to them, if they are under age.

3 a Do you have a video recorder? Do you use it to record programmes?
b Should teenagers aged 14 to 16 be allowed to watch films with an 18 rating? Why (not)?

adio waves 🎧

97-99 FM

adio 1 *plays rock music.*

RADIO

Virgin Radio *is a commercial radio station which plays rock music 24 hours a day.*

95.8 CAPITAL FM
L O N D O N

apital Radio *is a very successful local radio station. It broadcasts in the London area.*

The BBC broadcasts on five national and 39 local radio stations. Each of the BBC radio stations specialises in a particular type of programme: Radio 1 specialises in rock music; Radio 2 in popular music and light entertainment; Radio 3 in classical music; Radio 4 in current affairs, and drama; Radio 5 in sport and current affairs. Local radio stations put on programmes which interest people who live in that area.

Most people listen to the radio in the morning. They like background music while getting ready to go to school or driving to work. Radio 1 is still the most popular radio station with an average of 9.76 million listeners. It used to have many more listeners, but is now not so popular because of competition from 150 new commercial radio stations. Very few young people listen to any of the BBC radio stations: the top three radio stations for 15- and 18-year-olds are all commercial.

4 Which do you prefer, radio or TV? Why?

1 | a What's your favourite shop?
| b Where is your favourite shop?
| c Is your favourite shop a chain-store?

The High Street

In the centre of most towns and villages there is a main street with lots of different shops. This street is usually called the High Street. The high streets of Britain are beginning to look more and more the same. This is because they are full of branches of big chain-stores.

One of the best-known chain-stores is Marks & Spencer, which sells clothes and food. The company has over 700 stores world-wide and has a reputation for good quality. If you buy something that you decide you don't like, you can take it back and get your money back.

Marks & Spencer is a chain-store.

In most high streets there is a charity shop. All the profits from the things sold go to charity. Oxfam is the best-known chain of charity shops and it sells second-hand clothes and books.

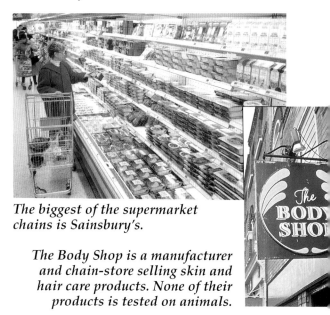

The biggest of the supermarket chains is Sainsbury's.

The Body Shop is a manufacturer and chain-store selling skin and hair care products. None of their products is tested on animals.

The corner shop

Eighty-seven per cent of British people live less than a mile from their local corner shop. A corner shop is a small shop on, or near, a street corner. Most corner shops sell food and newspapers.

Many are run by Indian or Pakistani families. The teenage children help their parents in the evening or at weekends. Corner shops are open until late in the evening, as well as on Sundays, so the people who run them work very hard.

Inside a corner shop.

Harrods

Department stores are found in all big cities. They are big shops where you can find almost everything you want and which offer a wide choice of things. The most famous British department store, Harrods, started as a small grocery shop in 1849. The present store has more than 300 departments and a staff of over 4,000 people. The display in the food hall is amazing. For example, there is a choice of over 500 types of cheese.

The food halls at Harrods sell all kinds of food products.

Street markets

Street markets are fun and cheap. Most markets sell fruit and vegetables, clothes, things for the house, records and jewellery. In London, there are about 40 or 50 markets. Some specialise in flowers, pets or second-hand books. Camden Lock Market in North London is very popular with young people. The stalls sell new and second-hand clothes, CDs and jewellery. Some towns are called market towns. A market is held there, usually once a week. People come from the surrounding towns and villages to do their shopping.

Stalls selling jewellery, hats and bags at Camden Lock.

Out-of-town shopping

Many small high-street and corner shops are closing down because people prefer to drive to a shopping complex outside town. About 8 per cent of people do all their shopping in a shopping complex, because they can park their cars easily.

In a British shopping complex, you usually find a supermarket, a branch of most of the chain-stores, some smaller shops, a few cafés and sometimes a multiplex cinema.

Most of the new shopping complexes are built near big roads, outside town. Here you also find superstores. These enormous shops sell their products more cheaply than in the high-street shops. Many of the superstores, such as IKEA or Aldi, are branches of chain-stores from countries outside Britain.

2 What do they sell?
a Sainsbury's
b Body Shop
c Oxfam
d a corner shop
e Harrods
f Camden Lock Market
g a shopping complex
h a superstore
3 Give examples of chain-stores in your country.

LEISURE *Sport*

1
a What is a spectator sport?
b Give an example of a team sport.
c Which sports do you associate with Britain?
d Can you name any important sports competitions which take place in Britain?

The British and sport

Britain does not often produce sportsmen or sportswomen who are successful in world sporting championships, but it has been good at inventing sports and writing rules of games.

Golf was first played in Scotland in the fifteenth century and the most famous golf club, Saint Andrews in Scotland, is still the most respected authority on golf in the world. Cricket was first played in England in the sixteenth century and its rules were written in the eighteenth century.

Football, rugby and hockey were first played in British public schools in the nineteenth century. The rules for all of these games were written between 1870 and 1890.

The rules for lawn tennis were first written in 1875

Football crazy

Every year there are 11.5 million attendances at League football games, making it one of the most popular spectator sports.

Britain's national sport is football. During the football season (August to May) most professional footballers play two matches every week. Some people say this is too many because the players do not have enough time and energy for international games.

The 22 best English teams play in the Premier League. The other professional teams play in Divisions 1, 2 and 3. Manchester United and Liverpool are two of the most successful teams. They have both been successful in many national and international tournaments.

The most exciting games are often between teams from the same city: Manchester United and Manchester City; Arsenal and Chelsea from London; Celtic and Rangers from Glasgow.

The highlight of the football season is the FA Cup Final at Wembley Stadium in London. Eighty thousand fans fill the stadium and there is usually a very good atmosphere.

Cricket

Cricket is a popular summer sport in England. It is not played much in Wales, Scotland and Northern Ireland, but it is very popular in the Commonwealth countries of Australia, India, New Zealand, Pakistan and the West Indies. Every year there are Test Matches between all these countries. A Test Match can last for up to five days. Usually Commonwealth countries play better and faster cricket than England. Many people think of cricket as a slow sport, but the ball can be bowled at speeds of up to 85 miles per hour (136 kph).

The ball goes past the batsman and hits the stumps. The batsman is out of the game.

Rugby

Rugby takes its name from Rugby School in the Midlands. In 1823, a boy playing football at the school picked up the ball and ran with it.

Rugby is a type of football. It is played with an oval ball and players can both kick or run with it. There are two types of rugby: in Rugby Union there are teams of 15 players, who are amateurs, and it is played by England, Wales, Scotland, Ireland (a joint team from both Northern Ireland and the Republic of Ireland), France, South Africa, Australia and New Zealand. There are regular matches between these countries. In Rugby League there are 13 players in a team, the players are all professionals and it is mostly played in the north of England and Australia.

MOST POPULAR SPORTS PLAYED BY WOMEN

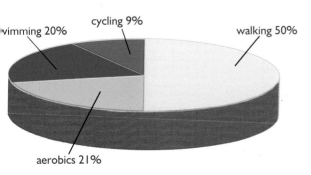

swimming 20%
cycling 9%
walking 50%
aerobics 21%

MOST POPULAR SPORTS PLAYED BY MEN

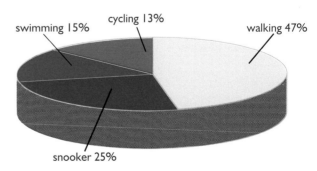

swimming 15%
cycling 13%
walking 47%
snooker 25%

2 a What are the most popular sports in your country?
Compare them with the most popular sports in Britain.
b Which of the sports mentioned in the text are played in your country?

LEISURE Free time

1 a Give an example of an individual sport.
  b Do you know the names of any famous British sportsmen or women?

Keeping fit

There are 2,000 sports centres in Britain: one for every town, large or small. They were built mostly in the 1980s to encourage the public to take part in sport. The number of people who take part in sport has risen, but not many people exercise more than once a month.

> I go mountain biking most weekends, usually with my mates. I've discovered loads of places on my bike. It's my favourite hobby.

The majority of people live in towns and cities, where space for team sports is limited. To keep fit, most people take part in individual sports. They usually go walking, swimming, cycling, or do aerobics. Taking part in all of these sports is informal and casual. Most people just want to relax. If they do aerobics or go swimming, they usually go to the sports centre, but not many people join a sports club.

Although many British people are interested in staying healthy, not many people do very much about it. A recent survey proved that many people were not as active as the thought and incorrectly believed that they did enough exercise to stay healthy. Only 10 per cent of adults take part in sport more than twice a week.

Aerobics

In the morning, many people follow fitness classes shown on TV. This is the fitness expert, Mr Motivator, who leads the classes.

2 Look at the list of classes available at the sports centre. Which class would you like to do?

JUBILEE HALL SPORTS CENTRE

MONDAY

TIME	CLASS	LEVEL	INSTRUCTOR
07.30 -08.30	Aerobics – Fat attack	advanced	Jamie
13.00 -13.45	Circuit training	all	Jo
13.50 -14.00	Step workout	beginners	Sara
17.30 -18.15	Step workout	advanced	Phil
18.00 -18.45	Circuit training	intermediate	Sara
18.45 -19.30	Aerobics – Fat attack	beginners	Sally
19.00 -20.00	Step workout	beginners	Rob

CLASS DESCRIPTIONS

Aerobics – Fat attack An aerobics class to lose weight on your hips and thighs.

Step workout A low impact workout, which does not h your ankles, knees or hips, using your st

Circuit training Use the weights and our large range of equipment to increase your strength.

FISHING

One of the most popular individual sports for men in Britain is fishing, also called angling. The most expensive type of fishing is for salmon and trout: these fish are only found in private rivers and lakes. Nearly 4 million anglers in Britain wait hours beside canals, rivers and lakes to catch a fish. Then they weigh it and usually throw it back into the water again.

British champions

In motor racing, Britain has had seven World Champion drivers. Successful British racing drivers include Eddie Irvine, David Coulthard and Damon Hill. There are also famous British racing car designers.

*hletics is a very popular spectator
*ort in Britain. Sally Gunnell won
ces in the European,
*mmonwealth, World and Olympic
*0-metre hurdles.

Chris Boardman won a gold medal for cycling at the 1992 Olympics, then became a professional road racer. Graeme Obree broke the world record in 1993 by riding 52.27 kilometres in one hour.

3 Describe one of the sports mentioned in the Sport and Free time pages. Don't forget to answer the following:
  a Is it a team sport or an individual sport?
  b Is it popular in Britain?
  c What equipment do you need to play it?
  d Who is the champion?
4 What is your favourite sport?

63

1 | What do you think the following words mean?
  a pub sign   **c** lamp-post   **e** shop front
  b pillar box   **d** bench   **f** telephone box

Signs in the street

You can see the history of Britain from the street. Pub signs, street names and even old shop fronts give you an idea of how old a town is, who its important people are and where and when they lived.

Small round blue signs on the front of buildings in London tell you which famous person used to live there.

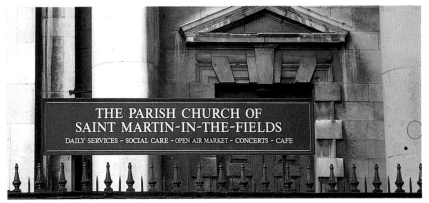

Names of buildings can give you an idea of what a place used to look like. There is a church in the centre of London called Saint Martin-in-the-Fields. It is now on Trafalgar Square, but when it was built in 1726 it was in the middle of fields, outside the old City of London.

Street names can tell you what kind of shops used to be there.

Many pub signs tell stories from British history. This pub sign shows King Charles I (right) and Cromwell (left) in an oak tree. Charles hid in the tree to avoid being captured by Cromwell (see page 11), but he was found and beheaded.

2 | **a** Look at the blue sign. Who lived there? When did he live? What did he do?
  b Describe the pub sign. Guess the name of the pub.
  c Do you know any place names which celebrate important moments in your country's history?

street furniture

The famous red telephone box (above left) was designed by Sir Giles Gilbert Scott in the 1920s and 1930s. In 1985, most were replaced by modern telephone boxes (above right). The public protested so much that the old ones were put back in London's main tourist areas.

*If you want to post a letter in Britain, there are over 100,000 letter boxes. The first pillar boxes appeared in 1853. You can tell that this pillar box was made when Queen Victoria was on the throne (1837–1901). The letters **VR** stand for **Victoria Regina** (Latin for Queen Victoria).*

This lamp-post, whose base is made in the shape of a dolphin, was also built when Victoria was Queen. At first it was a gas lamp, but now it works using electricity.

*These benches beside the River Thames are decorated with camels. They are near an old Egyptian monument called **Cleopatra's Needle**. The needle was given to Queen Victoria by Khedive Ishmael of Egypt. It was brought to London in 1847.*

3 **a** Describe the telephone boxes. Which style do you prefer and why?
b Describe the pillar box. When do you think it was made?
c Do you like the benches? Why (not)?

4 **a** What street furniture, new or old, is there in the main street of your town?
b Does the street furniture in your town tell you when it was built?

1 a How many different forms of transport can you use to get around town?
 b Which forms of transport are best and worst for the environment?
 c Give examples of any problems you have getting around your home town.

The London Underground

The first underground railway system in the world was in London. It opened in 1863 and ran 4 miles (6.5 km) from the west of London to the City in the east. The first lines were built close to the surface and used steam trains. Then they built deeper tunnels and the electric underground railway opened in 1890. This system was called the *Tube*, still the most popular name for the London Underground. Some of the Tube stations are so deep that they were used as air-raid shelters during the Second World War when hundreds of families would spend the night in the stations.

One million people commute into central London every day. Sixty per cent of these people use the Tube, mainly because the London Underground system extends far into the suburbs. The Northern Line, running from north to south, covers 18 miles (28 km); the Piccadilly Line, running from east to west is 47 miles (76 km) long.

WATERLOO

This sign shows the entrance to a station on the London Underground.

UNDERGROUND

TO

ANYWHERE

QUICKES

WAY

CHEAPES

FARE

NO NEED TO ASK A P'LICEMAN!

This poster advertises the first London Underground map which was introduced in 1908. The second design in 1933 wa more popular and it is still used today. Maps for transport systems in other countries used the London design as a mod

Taxis

London taxis are also called black cabs.

London taxis search the centre of the city for passengers. Taxis are often called cabs, from the French word *cabriolet*, which is the nineteenth-century word for a coach drawn by a horse.

Taxi-drivers, or cabbies, are proud of their knowledge of London. They have to know every street in central London – all 113 square miles (292 km^2) of it – and spend up to four years learning the best routes. To get a licence, they have to pass tests, known as "the Knowledge", until their answers are absolutely accurate. Because of this long training period, cabbies are often angry that people can drive minicabs without a licence. Minicabs do not have meters and look like normal cars. They cannot pick up passengers in the street, so people have to phone for a minicab.

THE DOUBLE-DECKER BUS

Most London buses are red. In one year, London's buses travel 163 million miles. That is all the way to the Sun and ¾ of the way back! Buses in London are not as popular as the Tube because they get stuck in traffic. London traffic now moves at an average of 6 miles per hour, the same speed as when there were horse-drawn coaches.

Alternative forms of transport

One of the most popular forms of urban transport in Britain used to be the tram. They were first used in London in 1861, but they were all replaced by buses after 1945. Trams are making a comeback. South Yorkshire has a 19-mile (30-kilometre) Supertram network which opened in 1994. Many cities are considering trams as alternatives to buses. Manchester uses trams as part of its Metrolink system, which goes across the city centre to link up towns on each side. The Manchester trams are clean and quiet and carry up to 250 people each. They do not get stuck in traffic. So far the Metrolink system has reduced car trips by an estimated 2 million a year, which is 10 per cent of the total car journeys every year.

Manchester trams have no steps so they are easy to use if you are disabled, have a pram or are carrying lots of shopping.

Cycling can be unhealthy: pollutants from cars, buses and lorries can affect your breathing. Many cyclists in cities wear masks to protect themselves from the exhaust fumes.

The most environmentally friendly vehicle is a bicycle, but cycling in Britain can be dangerous as there are not many bicycle lanes in British cities. Many drivers do not realise that there are cyclists on the roads: cyclists, like pedestrians, are almost as likely to be killed or injured as motorists. This is why an increasing number of cyclists wear helmets and fluorescent clothing.

2   **a** Is cycling encouraged in your home town? In what ways?

     b List all the forms of transport in your home town. Give each transport system a number between 1 (very bad) and 10 (excellent) in each of the following areas: noise, cost, convenience, frequency, safety, exhaust fumes. Discuss your results in groups.

GETTING AROUND *On the road*

1 **a** Does your family have a car? more than one car?
   b How often do you use the car?
   c Which form of transport is the cheapest in your country?

Traffic

The British love their cars: 45 per cent of families own one car and 25 per cent have two or more cars. Statistics show that people are using their cars much more, especially to go to work. It is estimated that traffic on all roads will double during the next 30 years. About 10 per cent of people walk to work; not many cycle, because it seems too dangerous. For many commuters public transport seems expensive and not very convenient.

It is not surprising that travel by car is so popular. If you want to travel from London to Oxford by train, a return ticket for one person costs four times as much as the petrol for a car which can take you and three friends.

Rush hour on a British motorway.

Protesting against road-building

Protesters trying to stop a new road being built through an ancient wood.

Britain in the 1980s and early 1990s, had a large road-building programme, but experience showed that more roads led to more traffic problems.

An increasing number of people, not just "green" activists or left-wingers, want money to be invested in public transport rather than new roads. They protest against the number of roads being built. In February 1994, 600 police were needed to end a demonstration against a motorway extension. The extension would have destroyed 300 houses to save 11 minutes' driving time.

The protests have forced the Government to abandon some of its road-building programme.

3 Using the text and the photos choose the best way to travel for the following people. Give reasons for your answers.
   a A 16-year-old has to get to school every morning and there is no bus service.
   b Four students want to go to Oxford from London. One of them has a car.
   c A student, who lives in London, wants to go to a big party in Oxford. She has got a car, but she wants to drink.

4 Do you think the penalties in Britain for drinking and driving are reasonable?

Road safety

In spite of having such dense traffic, Britain has one of the lowest number of road deaths in Europe. A large number of the people at risk from car accidents are pedestrians, especially the very young and older people.

There are a number of reasons for this. Seat-belts must be worn by drivers and all passengers. Most people remember to put on their seat-belts. There are strict rules against drinking and driving. A person found driving over the alcohol limit can be banned from driving for two or three years, fined heavily (up to £5,000), or even sent to prison. On motorways, there is a speed limit of 70 miles per hour (112 kph).

This poster tries to make people aware of dangers of drinking and then driving.

Look her in the eye. Then say a quick drink never hurt anybody.

DRINKING AND DRIVING WRECKS LIVES.

Learning to drive

You have to be 17 before you can drive a car, but you can ride a moped when you are 16. In Britain, you can learn to drive a car by taking lessons with an instructor or any experienced driver. This means that learning to drive is not too expensive. A lot of young people learn to drive in their parents' car. There is also a written part to the driving test, which you have to pass before you can take the driving part of the test.

My mum taught me how to drive. I passed my driving test when I was 17 - first time!

This is an L plate (pronounced "ell plate"). Learners must put it on the back and front of the car, if they have not yet passed their driving test.

E84 MHT

2 What are the differences between the driving test in your country and in Britain?

COACHES

Coaches are long-distance buses. Travelling by coach is cheaper than by train: most tickets cost 70 per cent of the equivalent train fare. Because of the difference in price, about 10.5 million people a year use the coach. Coaches go to more remote or isolated places than trains.

511 LONDON

NATIONAL EXPRESS

1 **a** How often do you travel by train?
b Define the word *commuter*. Use a dictionary to help you.

Commuting to work

Many people in Britain live a long way from their work. They often travel by train from the suburbs into the town centre to work. These people are commuters. Some people travel more than 200 miles every day and spend up to two hours going to work and two hours going home. Train tickets may appear to be expensive (£2,500 a year for an annual season ticket from Brighton to London), but this form of transport is a fast and environmentally friendly alternative to using a car.

On some trains, there are study clubs which offer language lessons to commuters on their way to and from work.

Let the train take the strain. People who don't drive to work are able to read a newspaper or a book. Some commuters even get out their laptop computers and work

The trains which run on main line routes are Intercity 125s (one-two-fives) or 225s (two-two-fives). 125s travel at 125 miles per hour (201 kph) and 225s travel at 140 miles per hour (225 kph).

Changes

Welcome to Waterloo
This station is owned and managed by
RAILTRACK

Great Western
Train services are provided by
REGIONAL RAILWAYS South Wales and West
SWT SOUTH WEST TRAINS

The organisation of the railway system in Britain has changed recently. For many years the railway was run by a public company, British Rail. In 1994, this company was split into two parts: Railtrack, which owns the track and the stations, and several private companies, which operate the trains.

Some people are worried about the change. They believe that private companies will only run one or two trains a day to small country villages or that they will close village stations.

This sign at the entrance to Waterloo Station in London shows that the railways are now privatised.

Train spotting

Train spotters are fans of trains. You can see train spotters at many train stations. They stand at the end of the platform and spend hours writing down the numbers of the trains. Serious train spotters travel thousands of miles by train trying to collect the number of every train in Britain.

ROYAL SCOT

FLYING SCOTSMAN

Some train spotters prefer old-fashioned steam trains. These stamps celebrate two famous steam trains.

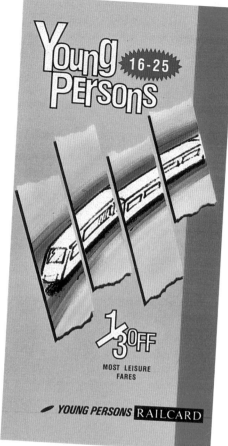

Young Persons 16-25

⅓ OFF

MOST LEISURE FARES

YOUNG PERSONS RAILCARD

2 Look at the leaflet.
a How old do you have to be to get a railcard?
b How much money do you save on fares?
c Do you think the railcard is a good idea? Why (not)?

Waterloo International Station in London opened in 1994. If you travel by train direct from Paris or Brussels to London, you arrive at this station. The station, designed by Nicholas Grimshaw, has won many architectural awards.

Children from Boothville Middle School entered a competition and won a free school trip to Paris on the Eurostar.

1 **a** Describe the photographs.
b What do you think is the best way to discover the countryside?
c What can you do in the countryside to earn a living?

Walking along the Pembrokeshire Coastal Path in Wales is a good way to enjoy the scenery.

Calderdale is part of the Pennine Way, one of Britain's well-known long-distance footpaths.

This wood in Hertfordshire is only one hour north of London.

Discovering the countryside

England is densely populated, but just outside the towns it becomes a country of green fields, low hills, rivers, small woods and leafy lanes.

At weekends, many British people like to discover the countryside and walk small parts of the long-distance footpaths which cross Britain.

The most well-known long-distance footpath is 874 miles (1,408 km) long and runs from Land's End, the south-west tip of England, to John o'Groats in the far north of Scotland. There is also the 248-mile (400-kilometre) Pennine Way, which starts in Derbyshire, in the centre of England and runs north to Scotland. The Pembrokeshire Coastal Path follows the coast in south-east Wales, and the Ridgeway, a pre-Roman path, runs from central England to the River Thames.

2 **a** Which long-distance footpath would you most like to do?
b A friend is coming to stay. S/he wants t spend a weekend discovering a beautif part of the countryside. Choose one are mentioned in the text to visit.
c How would you discover the area you have chosen?

Travelling by water

A relaxing way to see the countryside is by water. Britain has a large number of canals, which were used for transporting goods in the nineteenth century. About 2,000 miles (3,000 km) of canals are still in use.

Most canals are now used by holiday-makers who hire barges. Rivers, too, are popular. The River Thames, in particular, is full of private boats and pleasure boats. Imagine gently drifting along the river on a sunny summer day, past green fields; much better than being stuck in a traffic jam behind a huge lorry!

These canal boats are called barges or narrow boats.

The National Trust

The National Trust is a charity set up in 1895 to preserve places of historic interest and natural beauty in Britain. It owns 200 houses and 230 gardens, which it opens to the public. The Trust also protects 604,160 acres (2,445 km²) of the most beautiful countryside in Britain, as well as 575 miles (925 km) of coastline. Prehistoric and Roman sites, nature reserves, beaches, lighthouses, castles, even whole villages and islands are part of the Trust. It is one of the largest independent landowners in Britain. Many historic buildings are given to the Trust by people who want to make sure that the buildings are protected. In their spare time, volunteers help the National Trust to care for buildings and countryside.

3 Look at the poster for National Trust volunteers.
  a What are the people doing?
  b Would you be a volunteer? Why (not)?

VOLUNTEERS

Volunteers dry-stone walling in Gloucestershire

VOLUNTEERS ARE THE LIFE-BLOOD OF THE NATIONAL TRUST. EACH YEAR OVER 20,000 PEOPLE OF ALL AGES CONTRIBUTE MORE THAN A MILLION WORKING HOURS TO A WIDE RANGE OF CONSERVATION PROJECTS.

Changes on the farm

Britain is now a highly industrialised country and there are only 238,000 farms in the UK. More and more farmers leave the land because they cannot earn enough money to survive. Only large farms are economic and because of this most British farms are big. They usually grow cereals in the east of England and raise sheep and cows in the north of England and Scotland. The small family farms often have to earn more money by offering bed and breakfast accommodation to tourists.

Farming methods in Britain have also changed. Fields used to be quite small, divided by hedges which were sometimes a thousand years old and full of wild flowers and birds. Many hedges were pulled up to allow farmers to use modern machinery. Now most fields in England are large by European standards. Ironically, even though Britain is not self-sufficient, the European Union has asked all large farms to limit the amount of food they produce, so many English fields are now not farmed at all.

4 Describe a typical farm in Great Britain.

1 **a** Read quickly what people say about environmental issues in Britain.
b Which ideas do you agree with?

Recycling ∩

> Britain doesn't really care about its environment. Only 5 per cent of waste is recycled anyway. You can only recycle paper and glass and bins are always overflowing.

> But British people are concerned about the environment. I, along with 1½ million others who belong to conservation groups, spend our free time cleaning up beaches and looking after wildlife.

Roads ∩

> But this bypass destroyed Twyford Do a beautiful valley with two water meadows, which were Sites of Specia Scientific Interest (SSIs). The wate meadows were protected by European but they still built the bypass. The reason? To avoid some traffic-lights the edge of a town.

> I live in Lewes, in south England. For years we asked for a bypass because so much heavy traffic went through our town. It was shaking the foundations of 400-year-old buildings in the High Street. The lorries especially caused dreadful noise and air pollution, not to mention the number of accidents.

Animal rights 🎧

People in Britain are obsessed with conditions in which animals are kept. Why don't they worry about the conditions in which many people live?

I decided to join an animal rights group after seeing a television programme which showed the conditions in which battery hens were kept. They were in tiny cages. They could not move at all and their beaks had been removed. They were force-fed and injected with hormones to make them grow faster.

Energy 🎧

I am against the use of nuclear energy. The waste products can last hundreds of years. Even the Government, which invested a lot of money in nuclear energy in the 1980s, has been forced to admit that it's not a good idea. On the other hand, coal and oil pollute the air. I believe that we should look for other forms of power.

I live in Lancashire, in north-west England. The Government built some wind farms on the side of a hill, near to where I live. I am absolutely against this idea. The windmills spoil a beautiful area. They also make the most incredible noise, in an area which was always so quiet.

2   **a** What products can you recycle in your country?

b What conservation groups are there in your country?

c Are many people in your country against road-building plans? Why?

d Are you a member of an animal rights group? Why (not)?

e Do you think wind power is a good source of energy?

f What sources of energy does your country use?

3 Compare your answers with the opinions given in the text. Does your class/country have different ideas about the environment compared to Britain?

REGIONS London

1 a Write down three facts that you know about London.
   b Look at the photos. How many of the places or buildings do you recognise?

The history of London 🎧

◀ *This is Tower Bridge, built in 1894. It is next to the Tower of London. The Tower of London was built by William the Conqueror about 1,000 years ago.*

◀ *The Monument was erected in 1677 in memory of the Great Fire of London which destroyed almost all the old city in 1666. The column is near the bakery where the fire started.*

This is what London looked like in 1840. Saint Paul's Cathedral is the tall building with the dome. The cathedral was designed by the famous architect Sir Christopher Wren to replace the church which had been destroyed in the Great Fire of London. ▼

London is where the invading Romans first crossed the River Thames. They built a city a square mile in size, surrounded with a wall and called it *Londinium*. This original site of London is now called the City of London and is Britain's main financial centre.

The City is only a very small part of London. In the eleventh century, London began to expand beyond the City walls when King Edward the Confessor built a huge abbey at Westminster. Even today, Westminster Abbey and the Houses of Parliament, as well as all the shops, cafés, theatres and cinemas of the West End, are in the City of Westminster and not in the City of London.

2 a Who and what do you associate with the following things?
   The Tower of London
   Saint Paul's Cathedral
   b Find out more about the Great Fire of London. Look in an encyclopaedia.

Things to see ∩

When the eighteenth-century writer, Doctor Johnson, wrote "... when a man is tired of London, he is tired of life!" he was sure that no one could be bored in London. There are hundreds of historic buildings, galleries and museums. People can enjoy the parks and street markets, over 80 theatres and even more cinemas.

To discover London it is best to start with a tour on a sightseeing bus. It's also fun to go on a guided walk. These are advertised in *Time Out*, a weekly magazine that tells people what is happening in London. The walks last up to three hours and have special themes, such as "Ghosts and Haunted Taverns", "Royal London – Palaces and People", "The Beatles London – Rock Routes of the Sixties".

3 Which guided walk would you like to do? Why?

The Millennium Dome in Greenwich, open throughout the year 2000, was built to celebrate the new millennium.

Village London ∩

Next to Hampstead Village is Hampstead Heath, a huge park with open countryside, lakes, trees and bathing pools.

The centre of London has many different areas. Each one has its own special character. In London's West End, the Covent Garden area is crowded with cafés, clubs and clothes shops. Soho has a lot of clubs and discos. One part of Soho has so many Chinese shops and restaurants that it is called Chinatown.

Knightsbridge has a lot of exclusive and expensive shops, as well as many of the embassies. Nearby Chelsea and Sloane Street are supposed to be the homes of trendy rich kids.

When you go outside the centre, there are many areas which used to be small villages. As the city expanded, these villages became part of the city, but they still managed to keep their village character. Hampstead, the best-known of the villages, is extremely expensive. It is on one of the highest hills in London.

Cheap and free London ∩

Some visitors say that London is an expensive city, but there are some things to do which do not cost a lot of money. Most museums are free and give free guided tours as well as lectures.

The Royal Festival Hall on the South Bank of the River Thames has free music in the foyer every lunchtime. The National Theatre, next to the Royal Festival Hall, also has free concerts in the foyer in the evenings. Some cinemas are cheaper on Mondays; others sell half-price tickets before 6 pm.

4 **a** Think of five questions to ask your partner about London.
b Answer your partner's questions.

1 Do you like museums? Why (not)?

London's museums

You can find out about dinosaurs at the Natural History Museum.

You can find out about the history of the cinema and TV at the MOMI museum.

There are so many museums and galleries in London that even people who have lived there for a long time do not know them all. Some are traditional museums, but many are now making their exhibitions interactive, or hands-on, to encourage people to touch and understand what is on display. At the Science Museum, visitors can carry out experiments. At the Natural History Museum, visitors can find out how to look for fossils on the beach. At the National Gallery, the country's main art gallery, visitors can call up paintings on computer screens, find out about them and then print out a plan with their location indicated. The Clink Prison Museum is a reconstruction of a seventeenth-century prison. Visitors can look at a typical cell and heavy leg irons and chains.

At MOMI, the Museum of the Moving Image, almost all the things on display move. You can see how the first film was made, listen to the latest stereo systems and watch the news from the 1960s. You can design your own cartoons, read the news on TV and fly like Superman over London. The museum is moving to a brand-new building, which opens in 2003.

2 Which museum would you prefer to go and see? Why?

Along the river

The Houses of Parliament are beside the River Thames. They burnt down in 1834 and were rebuilt in 1840–60.

Kew is a suburb in west London on the River Thames. The Royal Botanical Gardens are here. The Palm House at Kew was built in 1844 and is made from iron and glass. It is over 328 feet (100m) long and 32 feet (10m) high. Some of the tropical plants inside had to be taken out because they were too tall.

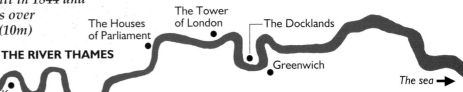

THE RIVER THAMES

The Houses of Parliament — Kew — Hampton Court — Oxford — The Tower of London — Greenwich — The Docklands — The sea ➡

Hampton Court Palace is outside London on the River Thames. King Henry VIII (1491–1547) lived here with his second wife, Anne Boleyn. The palace was built almost 500 years ago and is famous for its 300-year-old maze.

London used to be a very busy port, but the docks all closed in the 1960s when ships became too big to sail up the River Thames. The docks were redeveloped and new office blocks and flats were built there. Canary Wharf Tower (centre) is the tallest building in England.

The Cutty Sark at Greenwich on the Thames is a famous tea clipper. Tea clippers were fast sailing ships that brought tea from the Far East to Britain. The Royal Observatory is nearby. The zero longitude line runs through it and the time in every country in the world is calculated from this line.

3 | Make notes about things to see on the River Thames. You have one minute to tell your partner as much as you can about London and the River Thames.

1. Look at the map of Britain on page 2 for two minutes. Close your books. How many towns can you remember in the south of England? What do you know about them?

Lots of people 🎧

Nearly half of England's 49 million population is in the south of England. Most people live in London and the area around it (the South-East), because that is where most of the jobs are based.

Canterbury Cathedral in Kent is the home of the Archbishop of the Church of England. A fourteenth-century poet, Geoffrey Chaucer, wrote *The Canterbury Tales*, a collection of stories told by a group of pilgrims on their way to the town.

Kent is called the Garden of England, because a lot of fruit is grown there.

Bristol and Bath 🎧

These elegant Georgian terraced houses, built in the eighteenth century, are in the spa town of Bath.

The port of Bristol became rich in the nineteenth century by importing sugar, rum and tobacco and also by exporting slaves. It is still a rich city and is now the centre of the aviation industry. Rolls Royce makes aeroplane engines just outside Bristol.

The Roman town of Bath is near Bristol. The Romans settled there because of its natural hot spring, the only one in Britain. They built a temple to the goddess Minerva in front of the spring. In the eighteenth century, the town became popular with the Royal Family and the aristocracy. They came to bathe in the hot spring, drink the spa water from the fountain and socialise with their upper-class friends.

Sun worship at Stonehenge 🎧

People think that more than 3,500 years ago the huge stones of Stonehenge were transported 200 miles from Wales and set up in a circle on Salisbury Plain, a region south-east of Bristol.

Stonehenge is associated with sun worship: at dawn in midsummer, the sun rises exactly over a certain stone on the outside of the circle and shines onto the altar in the centre. Every year thousands of young people go to Stonehenge to take part in the midsummer Druid festival, but only a small number of people are allowed near the circle of stones. This has often led to violence with the police.

Some people think that the stones of Stonehenge were brought to the area by a glacier.

The south coast 𝄢

Brighton is the largest holiday resort on the south coast. It was once a small fishing village. In 1724, when the Prince Regent, later King George IV, started going to Brighton to swim in the sea, the town became very fashionable.

Further west along the coast is Bournemouth, also a holiday resort. Both Brighton and Bournemouth have many language schools, which give them a lively, cosmopolitan atmosphere, especially in the summer.

The Prince Regent liked Brighton so much that he built himself an Indian-style palace, the Royal Pavilion, there.

A ROYAL CASTLE

William the Conqueror began building Windsor Castle on a hill above the Thames 900 years ago. England's kings and queens have lived in it ever since. Parts of the castle were damaged in a fire in November 1992, but have been rebuilt.

The warm South-West 𝄢

The south-western tip of Britain, or the West Country, is the only region in Britain with an increasing population of young and old. It is the most popular tourist area for British people in the United Kingdom. It has the country's mildest weather and palm trees grow along the sea front of some holiday resorts in the counties of Devon and Cornwall. The Cornish fishing village of St Ives, has always attracted painters and a new modern art gallery was opened there in 1993.

The West Country also has three areas of wild, open countryside, known as moors. The largest of these is Dartmoor National Park. The moor is so isolated that in the nineteenth century a prison was built in the middle of it. Britain's worst criminals are kept there.

There are hundreds of little fishing villages on the south-west coast. A well-known one is St Ives on the north Cornish coast.

2 Which towns or places in southern England do you associate with the following?
  a English-language schools   **d** moors   **g** midsummer
  b aeroplanes   **e** spa   **h** holiday resort
  c fishing villages   **f** a royal castle

The Midlands and the North

1 Look at the map of the British Isles for two minutes. Close your books.
How many towns can you remember in the Midlands and the North of England?
What do you know about them?

Wool and cotton

Manchester is the second most important city in England. It is building several large sports stadiums and wants to host the Commonwealth Games in 2002. This is the new velodrome.

Wool has been associated with Yorkshire for centuries. Until the fifteenth century, wool from the North of England was sent to Flanders to be made into cloth. By the sixteenth century, the towns of Leeds and Bradford were themselves becoming important centres for wool and goods made from wool.

During the nineteenth century, Manchester became a very important centre for the production of cotton. It was even known as "Cottonopolis". Raw cotton came from the USA to the port of Liverpool, on the north-west coast. The cotton was transported by canal (after 1789) or by train (after 1830) to the nearby city of Manchester, where cotton goods were manufactured. They were then exported to the rest of the world.

No more heavy industries

The Industrial Revolution began in the Midlands. The Midlands and the North of England became the centre of the iron and steel industries. Newcastle became known for its shipbuilding and Birmingham became known for making cars.

Now there is no shipbuilding in Newcastle and there is only one major car company in Birmingham. Many towns in the Midlands and the North of England have high unemployment rates.

There are now only 16 coal mines in Britain and they are mostly near Nottingham. Britain used to have over 160 pits only ten years ago.

The Industrial Revolution began in the Midlands, at Ironbridge, just outside Birmingham.

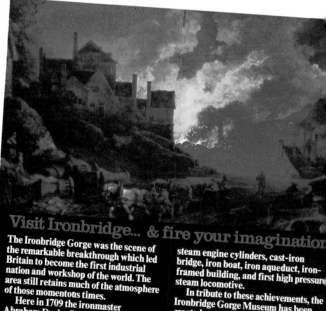

Visit Ironbridge... & fire your imagination

The Ironbridge Gorge was the scene of the remarkable breakthrough which led Britain to become the first industrial nation and workshop of the world. The area still retains much of the atmosphere of those momentous times.

Here in 1709 the ironmaster Abraham Darby first smelted iron using coke as a fuel, thus paving the way for the first iron wheels, iron rails, iron steam engine cylinders, cast-iron bridge, iron boat, iron aqueduct, iron-framed building, and first high pressure steam locomotive.

In tribute to these achievements, the Ironbridge Gorge Museum has been created around a unique series of industrial monuments spread over some six square miles of the Gorge.

Stately homes ◠

Aristocratic families and successful industrialists often built themselves beautiful country houses, called stately homes. Some of the most beautiful are in Derbyshire, a hilly county in the North-West of England.

Many stately homes are open to the public to help owners pay for them. Alton Towers, owned by the Earl of Shrewsbury, was developed in the 1980s into a theme park and is now the most visited paying attraction in the whole of Britain.

You can go on lots of rides at Alton Towers.

Foreign companies in Britain ◠

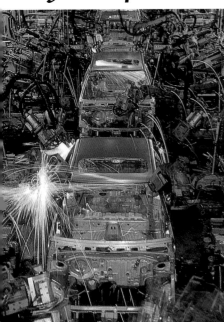

All major car manufacturers in Britain are owned by foreign companies.

Many foreign companies have opened factories in Britain. The Japanese car company Nissan opened a car factory near Sunderland in 1986. Nissan later became Britain's biggest car exporter, sending thousands of vehicles to 36 countries in the world. Toyota and Honda also have their main European factories in Britain. The Korean electronics company, Samsung, opened a factory in Sunderland in 1995. The foreign companies give jobs to many local people.

THE POTTERY INDUSTRY

Stoke-on Trent is famous for its pottery industry. Wedgwood makes the famous blue and white china.

2 Look at the leaflet for the Ironbridge museum.
  a What happened in 1709?
  b Where did the discovery happen?
  c Who made the discovery?
  d What happened after the discovery?
3 What do you associate with the following places?
  a Stoke-on-Trent
  b Manchester
  c Leeds
  d Birmingham
  e Sunderland
  f Alton Towers
  g Liverpool
  h Newcastle

REGIONS *Scotland*

1 True or false?
  a Scotland is a flat country.
  b The kilt is Scotland's national costume.
  c Scotland is a poor country.
  d Scotland has its own parliament.
  e Most people live in the Highlands.
  f Computers are made in Scotland.

2 Read the text to find out if you are right.

A tradition of independence

Hi. My name's Kirsty. I'm 17 and I'm from Glasgow. This year I'm taking six subjects for my end of school exams, Highers. My parents want me to go to a Scottish university because they think that standards are better than in English universities.

People in favour of Scottish independence say that the large quantities of oil found off the coast of Scotland are Scottish, not British, and the profits should go to Scotland.

Scotland has not always been a part of the United Kingdom. The Scottish people had their own royal family and fought the English for centuries. In 1603, King James VI of Scotland became King James I of England and Scotland. When he moved to London, Scottish independence ended.

In 1707, Scotland formally became part of the UK when the government of Scotland moved to Westminster, in London. Scotland managed to keep its own legal and education systems. Scotland still has different marriage laws from England. Young couples in England must have their parents' consent to get married if they are under 18, but in Scotland they can get married at the age of 16 without asking.

Scotland now has its own parliament in Edinburgh. The Scottish Parliament can decide on local matters and reduce tax a little. Some Scottish people still want their country to be completely independent.

Clans and tartans

Many Scottish names begin with "Mac" or "Mc", which means "son of". So the name "McDonald" means "son of Donald". Each clan or family name has its own tartan. The tartan is a checked cloth used to make the kilt, Scotland's national costume. Most people only wear their tartans for special occasions, like weddings and Burns' Night.

The Black Watch tartan and the Royal Stewart tartan are the most popular tartans. They are more popular with tourists than with the Scots.

The Black Watch tartan

The Royal Stewart tartan

Edinburgh, Glasgow and Aberdeen ∩

Visitors can look round Holyroodhouse in Edinburgh, the official residence of the Queen.

The Edinburgh Festival is an international Arts festival which takes place every August. It includes theatre, music, opera, dance, comedy and the Edinburgh Tattoo. The Fringe is the unofficial part of the Edinburgh Festival. More concerts and plays take place on the Fringe than at the official festival. ▶

Glasgow is the second-biggest city in Scotland. It used to have many shipyards. Now the shipyards have closed and smart houses with sea views have been built in the docks area instead.

Most of Scotland's 5 million population lives in or near Edinburgh, Glasgow or Aberdeen, where most of the jobs are. Scotland's traditional industries, such as coal, steel and shipbuilding have declined, but the Government has invested a lot of money in Scotland to develop it as an important European centre for computer production. Many large American and Japanese electronics companies have set up factories in southern Scotland and there are now many smaller Scottish companies which specialise in computer equipment. People have even started to call the area "Silicon Glen" (*Glen* is the Scottish word for valley). However, most of the high-technology parts such as chips and disk drives are still imported.

Highlands and Islands ∩

North of Edinburgh and Glasgow are the Highlands of Scotland: mountains with few trees, many sheep, wild deer and golden eagles. The Highlanders, the original people of the area, were removed by force by the English after their defeat at the Battle of Culloden in 1746. Many emigrated to America and Canada. Even today, few people live in the Highlands. Most of them are farmers, although there is also a lot of forestry and fishing. Large areas of the Highlands are kept by rich people for salmon-fishing and deer-hunting. Most Scotch whiskies are also made in the Highlands.

The Inner and Outer Hebrides are remote islands with small fishing and farming communities. Some of the people still speak Gaelic, the ancient Celtic language of Scotland.

Loch Ness is in the Highlands. **Loch** *is the Scottish word for lake. A monster is supposed to live in the loch. This photo of the monster was taken in 1934.*

1 a Wales is a Celtic country. Name one other Celtic country.
b What do you know about Celtic people and Celtic culture?

The Welsh language 🎧

Wales has a very strong Celtic culture. Many Celtic languages have almost disappeared, but Welsh is still used. Until 1825 about 80 per cent of the population spoke Welsh. During the nineteenth century there were fewer Welsh speakers, because many English and Irish workers moved to South Wales and Welsh people moved to the cities where less Welsh was spoken. At school, children were punished for speaking Welsh.

Recently, there has been more interest in Welsh. It is now spoken as a first language by more than 20 per cent of the population. It is used as a first language in more and more schools and it is studied as a second language in all other schools in Wales.

Welsh is recognised as a minority language by the EU and Wales receives money to help its language stay alive. There are television and radio stations with Welsh-language programmes, even soaps.

To understand how different Welsh is from English, compare these lines from the Welsh national anthem with their English translation.

Welsh
Gwlad! Gwlad! Pleidiol wyf i'm gwlad;
Tra môr yn fur i'r bur hoff bau,
O bydded i'r hen iaith barhau.

English
Homeland! I am devoted to my country;
So long as the sea is a wall to this beautiful land,
May the ancient language remain.

Both my great-grandmothers spoke Welsh. My father and his brothers could speak both Welsh and English, but all left Wales and married English women, so my generation speaks no Welsh. I'm learning it at evening class.

2 a Do any people in your country speak a different language from yours?
b Welsh is a different language from English, not a dialect of English. How is a dialect different from a language?
c Compare the situation in Wales with a region in your country.

A land of song 🎧

The Welsh have been famous for their singing for centuries. On his travels around Wales in the twelfth century, Giraldus Cambrensis wrote *"in a crowd of singers ... you will hear as many melodies as you see mouths"*. This tradition carries on today. If you go to a Welsh rugby match, you will hear supporters singing in harmony. Male-voice choirs are found throughout Wales, and many Welsh people have become famous opera singers.

The reputation of Wales as a centre for music attracts musicians from all over the world to its various festivals. Every year, 40 countries take part in the International Music Eisteddfod, and Wales' largest music festival, the National Eisteddfod, has performers from every country with a Celtic culture, including Scotland, Ireland, France and Spain.

The dragon is the symbol of Wales.

A land of castles and princes 🎧

Wales has not always been a part of Great Britain. Between the ninth and the eleventh centuries, Wales was divided into small states. In the thirteenth century, Llewelyn ap Iorwerth united the country and his son was crowned the first Prince of Wales. Welsh independence did not last long. Later that century, the English king, Edward I, conquered Wales and gave the title of Prince of Wales to his son, Edward. Since then the eldest son of the English king or queen has always been called The Prince of Wales and Wales is called a principality. Wales now has some self-government and its own assembly in Cardiff.

All over Wales there are medieval castles. They were built by the English to dominate the Welsh. There are so many of these medieval castles that they stretch like a chain across Wales. Perhaps the most impressive castle is Caerphilly. This huge fortress, dating from 1268, is one of the greatest surviving castles of the medieval western world.

Caernarfon Castle in North Wales. This is where Prince Charles, the heir to the British throne, became Prince of Wales in 1969.

Holidays in Wales 🎧

3 **a** What is the landscape like in Wales?
b What you would like to do if you visited Wales?

Many people go to Wales on holiday. It is famous for its mountains, which stretch from North to South Wales, its beautiful valleys and its national parks. In North Wales, visitors can go canal boating on the beautiful Llangollen Canal, or walking, pony-trekking and canoeing in Snowdonia National Park. In the South, there are wild, sandy beaches along Carmarthen Bay and around the Gower Peninsula. Most of its coast is protected and has not been spoilt by tourism or industry.

4 Look at this advert.
a How long does the train take?
b What can you see?
5 What is the landscape like in Wales?

SNOWDON MOUNTAIN RAILWAY ·LLANBERIS·

WELCOME

TIMES OF TRAINS
Trains do not run to a strict timetable. Weather permitting, and if there are at least 25 passengers, the first train of the day departs at 09.00 hrs. Trains run at frequent intervals until mid-afternoon.

JOURNEY TIMES
The train journey to the summit takes approximately one hour. Each train waits at the summit for ½ hour before leaving again for the descent to Llanberis. (2½-hour round trip).

FACTS & FIGURES
The railway is on the north-western slopes of Snowdon, the highest mountain in England and Wales. On fine days, the views from the summit are unsurpassed and the Wicklow Mountains of Ireland and the Isle of Man can be seen. Clear, sunny days cannot always be guaranteed and passengers are advised that the summit is frequently in the clouds and appropriate clothing should be worn.

Wales has many activity holiday centres where you can try canoeing, sailing, climbing, pony-trekking and mountain biking.

1 Which of these words do you associate with Northern Ireland?
a United Kingdom **e** peace
b IRA **f** UVF
c violence **g** mountains
d beauty **h** independence

Going back in history

The problems between Protestants and Catholics in Northern Ireland started a long time ago and are more political than religious.

For centuries the English had tried to gain control of Ireland. Until the sixteenth century, England controlled only a small area of Ireland around Dublin. English rulers, including King Henry VIII (1491–1547), Queen Elizabeth I (1533–1603) and Oliver Cromwell (1599–1658) gradually conquered the whole of Ireland. Ireland became an English colony in 1607.

The last area to resist the English was the province of Ulster, in the north of Ireland, but in the end the Irish were defeated. The English punished the Catholic people of Ulster for their resistance by giving their lands to Protestants from Scotland and England.

In 1921, an independent Irish state was set up, that is the Republic of Ireland. Six counties in the north of Ireland were dominated and controlled by Protestants, who refused to join the new Irish state. These six counties stayed part of the UK and are now called Northern Ireland.

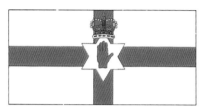

Ulster is the name used today for the six counties of Northern Ireland. The top flag represents these six counties. The bottom flag represents the original province of Ulster, which had nine counties.

The Troubles

From 1921 to 1972, Northern Ireland had its own parliament in Belfast, the capital. Politically and economically the province was controlled by Protestants, who were the majority of the population. In the late 1960s, there were large, peaceful demonstrations by Catholics who wanted better political representation, jobs and housing. Protestant reaction to the demonstrations was strong and often violent. In 1969, British soldiers were sent to Northern Ireland to help keep the peace.

In 1972, 13 Catholics were killed by British soldiers during a civil rights march. This incident, known as Bloody Sunday, led to even greater problems between Catholics and Protestants. This long period of violence since the 1960s was called the Troubles; more than 3,000 people died and 30,000 were injured.

Terrorist violence has been caused by the Irish Republican Army (IRA) on the Catholic side, and groups including Ulster Volunteer Force (UVF) on the Protestant side.

Talks between all the political groups, and including the British and Irish governments resulted in the Good Friday Agreement of April, 1998 and the possibility of a Northern Ireland parliament again.

Most people in Northern Ireland want a peaceful solution to the Troubles.

A land of beauty 🎧

Northern Ireland is a very beautiful place. It is a land of mountains, rivers and lakes. It has a rugged coastline and you are never more than half an hour away from the coast by car.

I like going to Lough Erne at the weekend. I go fishing. It's really peaceful. There's lots of wildlife you wouldn't see anywhere else.

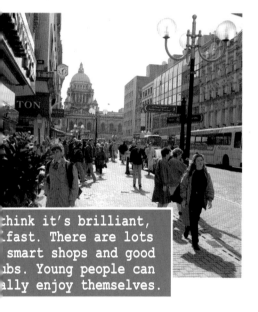

think it's brilliant, fast. There are lots smart shops and good bs. Young people can lly enjoy themselves.

Glenariff Forest Park, in the north-east — that's the loveliest area of all. You can't even begin to imagine the beauty of it.

Stories and myths 🎧

The people of Ireland have always been known for their stories and myths. They say that giants used to live on the Antrim coast, north of Belfast. One giant, Finn McCool, the commander of the king of Ireland's army, fell in love with a woman giant in Scotland. He wanted her to come to Ulster so he started to build a bridge, the Giant's Causeway, so that she could walk across the sea.

The Giant's Causeway is on the north coast. It is Northern Ireland's most famous natural attraction.

2 Look at the list of words in exercise one. How many of the words do you now associate with Northern Ireland?

Typically British

Before you listen ...

How much do you know about the British? Work with a partner.
Decide what you think should fill the gaps in these sentences:

1 British people live _____
_____
_____.

2 The traditional Sunday lunch in Britain is _____
_____
_____.

3 For breakfast, most people eat _____
_____
_____.

4 British people love _____
_____
_____.

5 The British weather is _____
_____.

6 The favourite drink of British people is _____
_____.

Now listen

A Juan and Paolo are asking Debbie about life in Britain. Listen to their conversation and find out how many things in the first activity you got right.

B Listen again and complete the questions:

1 Is it true that British people live in _____?
2 Do British people always have _____?
3 Is it true that British people are _____?
4 What about _____?
5 Do British people _____?

C Now write the answers from memory in your own words.

D Work with a partner. Write down three things that each of you thinks foreigners consider typical for your country. Discuss whether the stereotypes are right or wrong.

Speaking and writing

A Look at the photo, read the article and look up any words you don't know in the dictionary.

So, how do you take it, Ma'am, one's lump or two?

Queen stops for cuppa in Susan's council home

Using her best china, mum Susan McCarron lays on tea and biscuits for the Queen in an amazing scene yesterday.

Her Majesty popped into Susan's sparsely furnished council house during a visit to a sprawling Glasgow estate. Outside, scores of police were on patrol as a huge crowd of curious neighbours gathered and a fleet of five luxury limos waited.

B Answer the questions:

1 How many people are in the room? Who do you think they all are?
2 What do you notice about the room? Is it different from living rooms in your country?
3 Why do you think the Queen wanted to visit this house?
4 How are you supposed to address the Queen?
5 What do you think the Queen said to the owner of the council house?

C Here is a conversation that might take place between the Queen and the person she is visiting. Put the conversation in the right order and decide who says what. Then role-play the conversation with your friend. Take turns to play each part.

1 Thank you. I will. What a lovely room.
2 Good morning. Pleased to meet you.
3 Milk? Sugar?
4 Lovely to meet you too, Ma'am. Do come in and sit down.
5 Well, it's home. Can I pour you a cup of tea?
6 Milk, please, but no sugar for me.
7 Yes, please. Oh, chocolate digestives, my favourites.
8 Yes, please, I'd love a cup.
9 Would you like a biscuit?

D Prepare three questions you would ask the Queen if you met her.

E Has someone important ever come to visit you? Or has someone ever visited you unexpectedly? Write in your notebook about what happened.

The year in Britain

Before you listen ...

Work with a partner. Look at the pictures and match them with the sentences about some British festivals.

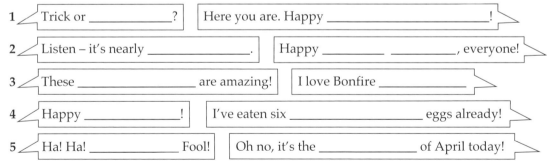

a On New Year's Eve, there are firework displays to welcome the New Year.
b On the fifth of November we remember Guy Fawkes and the gunpowder plot with fireworks and bonfires.
c At Hallowe'en, children dress in costumes as witches, ghosts or vampires, and go 'trick or treating'.
d One of the traditional Christmas desserts is a Christmas pudding.

Now listen

A Listen to the recording. You will hear five short conversations. Complete the speech bubbles below.

1 Trick or _____ ? | Here you are. Happy _____ !

2 Listen – it's nearly _____ . | Happy _____ _____ , everyone!

3 These _____ are amazing! | I love Bonfire _____

4 Happy _____ ! | I've eaten six _____ eggs already!

5 Ha! Ha! _____ Fool! | Oh no, it's the _____ of April today!

B Work with your partner. Look at each list. Say which is the odd one out and why.

1 trick   egg   vampire   witch
2 turkey   presents   decorations   fool
3 Big Ben   midnight   Valentine card   Auld Lang Syne
4 Fireworks   pantomime   bonfire   guy
5 tennis court   Wimbledon   ball   Brussels sprouts

C How many of the festivals on this page do you have in your country? Do you do/eat/drink the same things? If not, what do you do differently? Tell your partner.

Speaking and writing

A Find 12 vocabulary items about British festivals in the word search. The first one has been done for you.

B Write a sentence containing each of the words or phrases from the word search.
For example:
British people eat hot cross buns on Good Friday.

H	O	T	C	R	O	S	S	B	U	N	S	C	B	X	T
V	A	L	E	N	T	I	N	E	P	A	N	C	A	K	E
W	M	A	Y	D	A	Y	X	W	U	F	B	Y	I	T	F
I	A	S	C	O	T	O	R	M	A	Q	P	B	L	O	O
T	C	R	E	T	H	E	P	R	O	M	S	O	D	T	O
C	R	U	F	T	S	M	R	K	K	Q	S	L	L	C	L
H	F	K	O	P	C	X	F	I	R	E	W	O	R	K	S
J	H	G	S	O	O	P	Z	M	S	H	E	N	L	E	Y
W	N	C	V	T	T	P	A	N	T	O	M	I	M	E	W

C Play a guessing game with your partner. Write down the name of a British festival or event but don't show it to your partner. Your partner has to guess what it is. Your partner can ask a maximum of three questions to guess the correct answer. Example:
Student A: When is this event held?
Student B: It's held in June and July.
Student A: Where does it take place?
Student B: In South London. ...

D Write a paragraph about your favourite festival and the reasons why you like it.

Begin like this:
My favourite festival is Christmas, because I love giving and receiving presents. ...

E Look at the Edinburgh International Festival programme for Thursday, 19 August. Look at each item. With your partner, decide if it comes under the category of music, dance, theatre or opera.

F Put this conversation in the correct order.
1 Let's see ... there's a chamber music concert.
2 Well, I'm not keen on opera. I'd rather go to a concert.
3 Well, we could try a ballet ... how about *Sleeping Beauty*?
4 Oh no! Not chamber music!
5 What about going to an opera?
6 *Sleeping Beauty* is fine! Let's go and buy our tickets.

G With your partner, look at the programme and decide which events you want to go to. Check the time of each event.

Thursday 19 August

8.00pm — Page 13
Pittsburgh Symphony Orchestra
Mahler
Mariss Jansons Conductor
Sponsored by the Royal Bank of Scotland

11.00am — Page 22
Quatuor Mosaïques
Mozart, Beethoven

1.05pm — Page 20
Lunchtime Talk
Britten's Rape of Lucretia

7.15pm — Page 3
The Rape of Lucretia
Britten – CONCERT PERFORMANCE
Scottish Chamber Orchestra
Donald Runnicles Conductor

10.30pm — Page 7
Les Disparates
Charmatz
EDNA Dance Company

5.00pm — Page 20
Conversations
Quatuor Mosaïques

7.00pm — Page 9
The Wake
Murphy
The Abbey Theatre. Dublin
Sponsored by Lloyds TSB Scotland

2.30pm — Page 8
The Meeting
Cunillé. Traverse Theatre Company

8.00pm — Page 8
The Speculator
Greig. Traverse Theatre Company
Supported by the Festival Muses

The British at home

Before you listen ...

What do you like doing when you are at home? Look at the list on the right and number your three favourite activities 1–3. Then look at how British people like spending their time at home. How does it compare with your favourite activities? Do you have anything in common? Discuss with a partner.

1	Watching TV	99% ☐
2	Visiting/entertaining friends and relations	96% ☐
3	Listening to the radio	88% ☐
4	Listening to records/tapes/CDs	78% ☐
5	Reading books or magazines	64% ☐
6	Gardening	48% ☐
7	DIY	44% ☐
8	Dressmaking/needlework/knitting	20% ☐

Now listen

A You're going to hear four people talking about their homes. With your partner, look at the photos and try to predict two activities that each person will say they like doing at home. Listen to the recording. How many of your guesses were correct?

B Now listen again and fill the gaps:

Dan

1 Dan lives in a _____ with his parents. They enjoy _____ in the garden. They often have _____ to stay at the weekend. They spend time _____, _____ to music, and _____ snooker.

Angie

2 Angie lives in a _____ with her mum and her brother. It's near to everything. They often _____ a video and have friends round for a _____. Angie likes _____ and luckily there's a _____ around the corner. She goes there at least _____ a week.

Neil

3 Neil lived in a _____ house but now he's homeless. At his hostel, he spends time _____ and _____ chess or _____. Sometimes he has to go _____. But he wants a _____ of his own.

Sally

4 Sally lives on a _____ with three other students. At home she has to _____ hard on her course. In the evenings she _____ in a restaurant to finance her studies. In summer, they like _____ in the river and their friends come round for _____ parties.

94

C Make a short list of activities you do at home:

1 In summer _____

_____

2 In winter _____

_____

D Talk to your partner and compare your lists. Now work with another pair, and compare their lists with yours. Which is the most popular activity to do at home? Which is the least popular?

Speaking and writing 💬 ✏️

A Read the clues and complete the grid:

1 A ... house has land around it.
2 A ... house has other houses attached at each side.
3 Young couples tend to live in ... rather than houses.
4 Many people dream of retiring to a country ... .
5 A ... is someone who rents a place to live.
6 British people are usually proud of their front ... .

B Look at these advertisements for homes for rent and answer the questions below.

a One bedroom, ground floor conversion, garden, spacious lounge, fitted kitchen, fitted bathroom, gas-fired central heating, close to Tube.

b Luxury, purpose-built flat in 1990s-built development. Two bedrooms, luxury bathroom with power shower, fitted kitchen with washing machine, fridge/freezer, microwave, large lounge with balcony, video-entry system, allocated parking.

c Excellent quality, fully detached house in private mews with electric security gates. Four bedrooms (master with en suite), family bathroom, large lounge, dining room, fully equipped fitted kitchen, utility room, cloakroom, integral double garage and driveway parking, garden.

d Three bedroom, terraced house, through lounge, fitted kitchen, ground floor bathroom, first floor WC, rear garden, double glazed.

1 Which of the homes has a garden?
2 Which accommodation has a video-entry system?
3 What extra security does the four-bedroom detached house have?
4 In which property is there a room with a balcony?
5 Which property doesn't have a garden?
6 Use your dictionary to check the meaning of:
luxury en suite / cloakroom / utility room / study / allocated parking / conversion / mews / integral garage / double glazed

C Imagine you are looking for a flatmate. Write a short advertisement for your own house or flat, like the ones above. Remember to mention any special features or equipment it has. Are there any special buildings / monuments / areas of interest / transport links nearby? Are there any security features?

At school

Before you listen ...

Work with a partner. Match each word or phrase below with its correct definition.

1 GCSEs

2 National Curriculum

3 Boarding schools

4 Grammar schools

5 Comprehensive schools

6 Timetable

7 Assembly

8 Registration

9 A levels

a You look at it to find out what lessons are on what day and the exact times each lesson begins and ends.

b Pupils in these schools spend nights as well as days there, and go home during school holidays.

c You do these exams when you are aged 16.

d You need three of these in traditional subjects to get a place at a university.

e You have to pass an examination at the age of 11 to get into one of these state-run schools.

f It was introduced in Britain in 1988 and tells pupils what they should be learning at each stage of their education.

g The whole school gets together in the school hall to listen to songs or talks, or to join in prayers.

h These are state schools which accept pupils of all abilities.

i When teachers check who is present at school.

Now listen

A Before you listen to the interview with Kerry, a fifteen-year-old secondary school pupil, write down three questions you think the interviewer will ask her.

B Now listen to the recording again and then say how many questions you predicted correctly.

C Finish the following sentences:

1 Kerry goes to a _____.

2 Kerry hasn't got exams in _____.

3 In Britain, the school day usually begins with _____.

4 In British schools you can have lunch _____.

5 Lessons usually finish at about _____.

6 Kerry's favourite things about school are _____.

D Now listen to the recording again. Write down all the questions in your notebook.
Then choose a partner and interview him/her using the questions.

E Work with a partner. Make up an ideal timetable for a week.
Then take turns and describe one school day to your partner.

Speaking and writing

A Write sentences about yourself and your school using the following words:
1 Favourite subject
2 Exams
3 School uniform
4 Single-sex schools
5 Homework

B Read this extract from Grove Comprehensive School's Home/School Agreement which shows the rights, responsibilities and rules of the pupils.

Rights	Responsibilities	Rules
I shall try to:- ★ come to school on time every day. ★ bring to school everything I need for the day. ★ take responsibility for my own learning – listen, concentrate and always do my best. ★ take responsibility for the way I behave.	★ be kind and helpful to others. ★ show respect for all members of the school community. ★ look after the school and keep it free from litter and graffiti. ★ look after equipment and treat other people's property with respect. ★ follow the school rules.	

C The Home/School Agreement consists of three parts. What the pupils should do, what the teachers should do and what the parents should do. Discuss with your partner and decide what items you could include for teachers and parents in the Home/School Agreement.

Example: *Parents shall try to see that their child arrives at school on time every day.*

D Do you have a Home/School Agreement? Discuss which rules are the same for your school and which rules are different.

E Now look at the Pupil Behaviour Code below and work with a partner.
Read through each statement together, giving your opinion.
Say what you like or don't like about them and what is the same or different at your school.

PUPIL BEHAVIOUR CODE

BE QUIET AND ORDERLY.
Follow instructions.
No shouting. No pushing.
No running in corridors.
Walk on the left.
Don't call out in classes.

ARRIVE ON TIME.
Not just for registration,
but for every lesson.

RESPECT EACH OTHER.
Be considerate.
Resolve conflicts peacefully.
No bullying.
No racist, no sexist comments.
No swearing.

RESPECT THE ENVIRONMENT.
No graffiti or vandalism.
Don't drop litter.
Keep the school clean.

COME EQUIPPED TO LEARN.
Bring what you need
for your lesson.
Leave valuables at home.
Wear uniform.

At work

Before you listen ...

A Read the sentences below and decide which jobs they are about. Choose from the box below. Make up your own definitions for the words that are left over.

1 A person who makes sure that law and order are maintained.
2 A person who takes orders and serves meals in a café or restaurant.
3 A person who plays records and chats on the radio or at discos or parties.
4 A person who diagnoses and treats illness and disease.
5 A person who helps young people to learn and educate themselves.
6 A person who helps a vet to treat sick or injured animals.
7 A person who services and repairs cars, vans and other vehicles.
8 A person who washes, cuts, styles and colours people's hair.
9 A person who reads the news on TV.
10 A person who writes articles for a newspaper or magazine.

editor	hairdresser
garage mechanic	DJ
traffic warden	chef
barber	newsreader
policeman/woman	bus driver
waiter/waitress	reporter/journalist
doctor	teacher
veterinary nurse	

B Work with a partner. Take turns making up definitions and guessing the job.

Now listen 🎧

A Melanie, 17, is applying for a holiday job. Listen to her job interview. Can you work out what job she is applying for?

B Listen to the recording again and complete the questions.

1 What are you _____ ?
2 Do you mind _____ ?
3 This job isn't _____ . Is that a _____ ?
4 Do you get on _____ ?
5 Do you mind _____ ?
6 What special _____ ?
7 Do you have any _____ ?
8 Are there any _____ ?

C Now read the above questions and answer for yourself. Compare your answers with those of your partner. Which of you is better suited to the job?

Speaking and writing

A Read the job advert and say whether the statements below are true (T) or false (F).

Summer Camp Managers

Here's your opportunity to spend a great July and August running your own Summer Camp for youngsters aged 7–16. The manager will be responsible for the safety of about 50 kids, so a knowledge of first aid is essential, as is a good sense of humour. Other requirements: a motivator with high energy levels, unlimited patience and kid empathy, plus prior management experience. The job entails for example organising sports events, hobby classes, games and excursions.

Telephone 01234 567 789 (Voice Mail)

1 The job is only temporary. ☐
2 You would be in charge of the camp. ☐
3 You need previous experience in management. ☐
4 It doesn't matter if you don't get on well with young people. ☐
5 You would need to be good at motivating people. ☐
6 You don't need a lot of energy for this job. ☐
7 You would enjoy this job if you are quiet and introverted. ☐
8 This would be a fairly boring job. ☐

B Work with a partner. Discuss which of the following qualities would be
a important; **b** useful in the job. Then rank the qualities in order of their desirability.

1 Artistic ability ☐
2 Mathematical ability ☐
3 Loud, clear speaking voice ☐
4 Ability to work on one's own ☐
5 Fair-minded; good at sorting out arguments ☐

6 Good with money ☐
7 Enjoy working outdoors ☐
8 Patient and kind ☐
9 Get on well with animals ☐
10 physically fit ☐

C Discuss with your partner what experience/qualities you would need for the following jobs:

1 Policeman/woman
2 Architect
3 Waiter/waitress
4 Nursery school teacher
5 Gardener

D Work with a partner. Role-play a job interview for one of the jobs above. Then swap roles.

Student A:
You are applying for a job. Try to persuade the interviewer that you are the right person for the job. Think about the interviewer's questions carefully and answer as well as you can without talking too much.

Student B:
You are interviewing student A for a job.
1 Ask him/her about personal details: name, age, etc.
2 Ask if he/she has the qualifications or skills for the job, for example a driving licence/teaching qualification/typing and shorthand, etc.
3 Ask if he/she is physically fit, good with animals/people or children, whether he/she has artistic/musical or mathematical ability.
4 Ask about any experience the applicant has had.
5 Why does he/she think they could do the job?
6 Explain any special job requirements, like unusual hours, having to wear a uniform, etc.

Eating out and entertainment

Before you listen ...

Work with a partner. What do you do for entertainment in the evenings or at weekends?
Read the list of things to do in your spare time. Then number them in order of preference, 1-10.
Compare your list with a partner.

1 Going to the cinema ☐
2 Eating out ☐
3 Going to the theatre ☐
4 Going to a concert ☐
5 Going for a walk in the countryside ☐
6 Cooking a meal at home for friends ☐
7 Dancing at a club ☐
8 Going to a party with friends ☐
9 Eating a takeaway meal – a curry or a pizza – at home with friends ☐
10 Renting a video to watch at home / with friends ☐

Now listen 🎧

A Listen to the recording and match the correct dialogue to the correct restaurant.

Dialogue 1 ☐
Dialogue 2 ☐
Dialogue 3 ☐

a **Brown's English Restaurant**

b **DELHI CURRY HOUSE**

c **Ristorante di Torino**

B Now list the foods below the correct restaurant.

veal with tuna fish sauce, risotto, popadums, roast beef, onion soup, roast chicken, meat biryani, vegetable lasagne, Bombay potatoes, bean soup, chicken tikka masala, tomato soup

Brown's English Restaurant	Delhi Curry House	Ristorante di Torino

C Read these sentences and say whether they are true (T) or false (F). Correct the false statements.

1 The two women had an Indian meal. ☐
2 The man and the woman had an Italian meal. ☐
3 The two men had a British meal. ☐
4 The two women wanted roast potatoes. ☐
5 The waiter in the Italian restaurant couldn't recommend any vegetarian dishes. ☐
6 The couple in the Indian restaurant didn't want any Bombay potatoes. ☐
7 Both people in the Italian restaurant had soup for their starter. ☐

D Discuss with a partner which of the above meals you would prefer to have had.
Draw up your ideal menu for a three-course meal in a restaurant in Britain. Compare your choices with your partner's.

Speaking and writing

A Do you like going to the cinema? Look at these jumbled up types of films. Unjumble the letters below to form words to describe the different types. Then match up the words with the film titles below.
Example: *Comedy – c*

1 ECYDMO _____   **a** *The Mummy*

2 ORRORH _____   **b** *Star Wars*

3 REILRTHL _____   **c** *Notting Hill*

4 NOCOTAR _____   **d** *Rugrats The Movie*

5 NOTCIA _____   **e** *Shakespeare in Love*

6 ARMENCO _____   **f** *Saving Private Ryan*

7 ENESICC NOCTIFI _____   **g** *Terminator*

8 RWA _____   **h** *Psycho*

B Use the words in 1–8 to fill the gaps in these sentences:

1 *The Simpsons* is my favourite _____.

2 I hate fighting so I never go to see _____ films.

3 I enjoy a comedy with a bit of _____ so I liked *Notting Hill*.

4 Ever since he saw *ET* he's always loved _____-_____ films.

5 Many people find _____ films like *The Mummy* too scary.

6 Boys seem to prefer _____ films.

7 More women than men watch _____ films.

8 Alfred Hitchcock made _____ , like *Psycho* and *The Birds*.

C Read the cinema advert and answer the questions:
1 Which film won an award for best foreign language film?
2 Which horror film could you see at Putney?
3 Where could you see the film *Matrix*?
4 What would you do if you needed more information about a film showing at one of these cinemas?
5 Would you be able to see *The King and I* in the evening?
6 What do you think CC Booking means?
7 Near which famous London square is the ABC Swiss Centre?

D With a partner, describe one of the films without saying the film's name. Your partner has to guess which one it is.
For Example:
It's a romance. You can see it at Hampstead and Putney.
(*Answer:* Notting Hill.)

E With your partner, plan an evening out. Choose a film you both want to see and decide what time you want to see it. Then decide what to eat and whether you want to eat before or after the film.

TV, radio and newspapers

Before you listen ...

Work with a partner. Match these TV programmes to the type of programme you think they are.

1 *Friends* ☐
2 *The Simpsons* ☐
3 *Neighbours* ☐
4 *Top of the Pops* ☐
5 *Parkinson* ☐
6 *It's only TV but I like it* ☐
7 *Tonight with Trevor McDonald* ☐
8 *Honey I shrunk the kids* ☐
9 *The Tour de France* ☐
10 *Lion Country* ☐

a News and current affairs
b Film
c Comedy
d Chat show
e Soap
f Game / quiz show
g Cartoon
h Sports programme
i Music programme
j Documentary

Now listen

A You're going to hear a TV announcer telling you about programmes on TV for three different days. Listen and answer the questions.
1 What follows the news on Friday at 6 o'clock?
2 What kind of programme is *Maisie Raine*?
3 Who appears as a guest on *Parkinson*?
4 Name one of the characters from *Sesame Street*.
5 What is the name of the comedy programme on Wednesday morning?
6 What sport is being played at Wimbledon?

B Now listen again and fill the gaps in the schedule.

1

FRIDAY
6.00 News
7.00 *Watchdog,* _____
      programme
____ *Top of the Pops,*
      _____ programme
9.00 News
9.30 *Maisie Raine,* detective
      show

2

6.00 _____
      Sesame Street, children's
      programme
____ *The Big Breakfast,* news
      and entertainment
9.00 *The Cosby Show,*
      _____
9.35 *Babes in Arms,*
      _____

3

_____
12.00 News & Weather
12.05 *Eastenders,* _____
____ Wimbledon, _____
6.30 _____

C Work with your partner. Say which three programmes you would choose to watch and which three you would avoid. Compare likes and dislikes with your partner. Then try to draw up a schedule for an evening's TV viewing that you would both enjoy.

Speaking and writing

A Complete the crossword:

ACROSS

6 *The Observer* is a … paper.

7 *Good* … is the name of a women's magazine.

8 *PC* … is a specialist magazine.

9 *The Sun* and *The Mirror* are this style of newspaper.

DOWN

1 *Sugar* is a magazine for … girls.

2 *Smash* … is a music magazine which both girls and boys buy.

3 *Evening Standard* is a … London newspaper.

4 *The Times* and *The Guardian* are this kind of newspaper.

5 … is the name of a women's magazine in Britain.

B Read the stories. Check any unfamiliar words in the dictionary. Then answer the questions.

Needles in Asda bread

Thousands of loaves have been stripped from the shelves of the Asda supermarket chain after some were found to have been deliberately contaminated with sewing needles.

Police launched an investigation yesterday into the Stockport-based bakery supplying the firm after a fourth needle was discovered.

ASDA HIT BY NEEDLES IN BREAD ALERT

THOUSANDS of supermarket customers were last night urged to return bread after Asda revealed some loaves had sewing needles in them.

The alert went out after at least four customers found needles in their loaves.

1 What food was removed from the supermarket shelves?

2 What was the name of the supermarket chain?

3 How many needles were found?

4 What did the supermarket chain ask customers to do?

C You are a reporter working on the Asda story. Write two questions you would ask of:

a The manager of the supermarket.

b An angry customer who found one of the needles.

c A police inspector dealing with the case.

D Now work in a group of four. Produce a radio report on the story. Play the roles of the reporter, supermarket manager, police inspector and angry customer. The reporter should introduce the story:

Start: *Good evening, I'm … in … where … (say what has happened).*
(Now introduce your eyewitness and ask him/her some questions.)
Write linking sentences to introduce each person.
Example: *"We spoke to Detective Brown, the police inspector dealing with the case"*, etc.
Practise the report and present it to your class.

Sport in Britain

Before you listen ...

Find seven different sports in these jumbled up words and write them down.

B O T A O L F R I E T C C K R G Y B U F L G O G F H I I N S N E T I N S S I G W M N I M

1 _____
2 _____
3 _____
4 _____
5 _____
6 _____
7 _____

Now listen

A You're going to hear five people talking about the sport they do. Which sport is each person talking about? While you listen, tick the correct box in the exercise above.

B Now listen again and fill in the words associated with each sport.

1 I'm c_____ f_____ and last week I s_____ three g_____.

2 When we c_____ one, we w_____ it and t_____ it back in.

3 If it r_____ the m_____ is c_____ off.

4 It's f_____ to play d_____ m_____.

5 I carry my c_____ on a sp_____ tr_____.

C Do you play sport? Are you one of the 10 per cent of people who play sport more than twice a week? What are the most popular sports in your family? Interview your partner about the sports he/she and his/her family play.
Then interview the students in your class and produce a survey about the most popular sports in the class.

Speaking and writing

A Work with your partner. Answer these quiz questions:

1 Wimbledon is:
   a a tennis tournament ☐
   b a football match ☐

2 If you were at St. Andrews, you would probably be playing:
   a cricket ☐
   b golf ☐

3 What two British universities take part in the annual Boat Race?
   a Oxford and Cambridge ☐
   b Oxford and London ☐

4 Arsenal and Tottenham Hotspur are both football teams from:
  a Manchester ☐
  b London ☐
5 Golf was first played in:
  a the 15th century ☐
  b the 19th century ☐
6 Damon Hill was a famous British:
  a racing driver ☐
  b footballer ☐

B Now make up a quiz of your own. With your partner, try your questions out on another pair. Swap roles. Which pair has the highest score?

C Read the leaflet below and answer the following questions.

LEISURE CENTRE ACTIVITIES

Monday	4.30–5.30	**Girls gymnastics 9–12 years**
	5.30–6.45	**Gymnastics 12–Adult**
Tuesday	6.15–7.15	**Judo 5–12 years**
	7.15–8.15	**Judo 12–Adult**
Wednesday	6.00–8.30	**Netball**
	5.30–8.30	**Table tennis**
Thursday	4.00–5.30	**Badminton**
	6.15–7.15	**Aerobics**
	7.15–5.15	**Aerobics**
Friday	6.00–7.00	**Karate**
	4.15–5.15	**Trampoline 5–8 years**
	5.15–6.15	**Trampoline 8–12 years**
	6.15–7.15	**Trampoline 12–16 years**
Saturday	10.00 am–12.00	**Football** **Coaching every Saturday**
	12.00–2.00	**Badminton**

1 When are the trampoline lessons?
2 What activities are on Thursdays?
3 When are the table-tennis lessons?
4 For which age group is the judo lesson on Tuesday from 6.15?

D Imagine you want to do some sports at your local sports centre. Choose a partner and act out a role-play. Then swap roles.
Student A: You want to have trampoline lessons. Go along to your local sports centre and ask for information.
Student B: You work at the reception desk of a sports centre. Part of your job is giving people information about courses and facilities.

E Now work with a partner. You are keen to do a sports activity together, but you're not free on Mondays and your partner isn't free on Fridays. Look carefully at the leisure centre leaflet and choose an activity you both enjoy.

Travelling in Britain

Before you listen ...

Look at the speech bubbles and decide whether you would hear these phrases if you were travelling by car, train or bus. Write the correct transport in the gap.

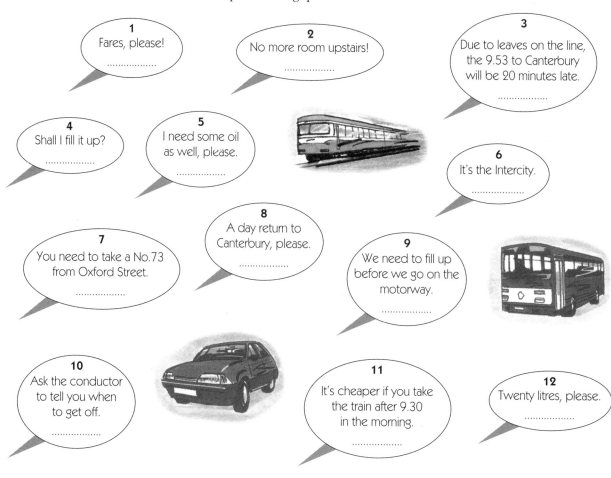

1 Fares, please! ....

2 No more room upstairs! ....

3 Due to leaves on the line, the 9.53 to Canterbury will be 20 minutes late. ....

4 Shall I fill it up? ....

5 I need some oil as well, please. ....

6 It's the Intercity. ....

7 You need to take a No.73 from Oxford Street. ....

8 A day return to Canterbury, please. ....

9 We need to fill up before we go on the motorway. ....

10 Ask the conductor to tell you when to get off. ....

11 It's cheaper if you take the train after 9.30 in the morning. ....

12 Twenty litres, please. ....

Now listen

A Now listen to the recording to check your answers.

B Listen again and say whether these statements are true (T) or false (F). Correct the false ones.
1 You can buy bus tickets on the bus.
2 You can't buy oil at a service station.
3 Buses are sometimes delayed by leaves.
4 It's more expensive if you travel after 9.30 in the morning.
5 Bus conductors don't help passengers.
6 You usually buy petrol in pints.

C How do you prefer to travel in your own country? Why? Which methods are cheaper/quicker/easier/dangerous etc? Make notes then tell your partner.

Speaking and writing 💬 📝

A Play the Manchester-Blackpool race game with three people. You need one dice and three counters. Throw a six to start, then throw again to find how far you can go.

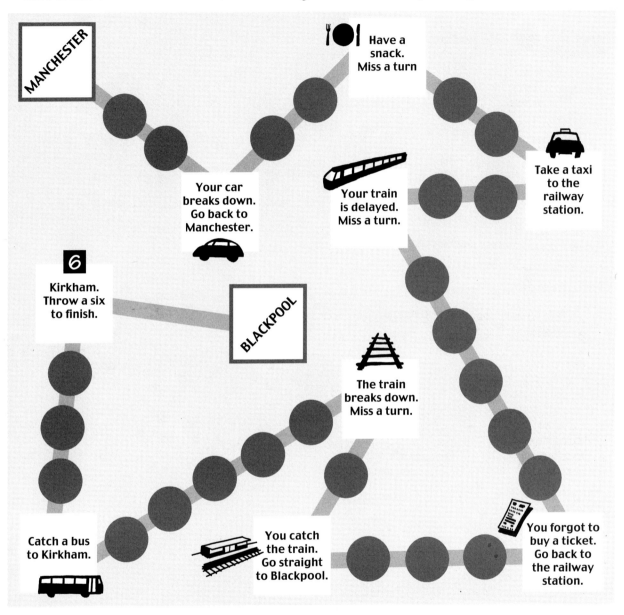

MANCHESTER

Have a snack. Miss a turn

Take a taxi to the railway station.

Your car breaks down. Go back to Manchester.

Your train is delayed. Miss a turn.

6 Kirkham. Throw a six to finish.

BLACKPOOL

The train breaks down. Miss a turn.

Catch a bus to Kirkham.

You catch the train. Go straight to Blackpool.

You forgot to buy a ticket. Go back to the railway station.

B Work in a group of four. Answer these questions:
1 At what age are you allowed to drive in your country? Is this too young/old? What do you think is the ideal age?
2 Is the driving test in your country too easy/difficult? Does it have a theory section as well as driving practice? How long does it last? What do you think is the ideal driving test?
3 What are the penalties for drinking and driving in your country? Are they strong enough? Are they too strong?

C Have you or has anyone you know ever been involved in a road accident, either as a pedestrian or in a vehicle? What happened? Could the accident have been avoided? How? Write about what happened in your notebook.

London

Before you listen ...

Look at these words and find eight pairs of words that are connected with London. Then match each one with its definition.

Great   MI   Dome   Westminster   Fire   London

Hampstead   Underground   Millennium

Abbey   Out   Kew   Time   Gardens   MO   Heath

1 A park next to one of London's famous villages. _____

2 It houses exhibitions and is in Greenwich. ____ _____

3 It destroyed the City of London in 1666. _____

4 It was built in the 11th century. _____

5 It gives information about entertainment in the capital. _____

6 You can see tropical plants here. _____

7 The Museum of the Moving Image. _____

8 It's also known as the 'Tube'. _____

Now listen

A Now listen and check your answers.

B Listen again and find out:
1 Who wins the quiz?
2 How many points did each person have?

Write the answer here: Emily had _____ points and Joe had _____ points so _____ was the winner.

C Now complete these sentences:

If I went to London, I would visit _____.

I would stay _____.

As a souvenir of my stay, I would buy _____.

I would go to _____.

Compare your sentences with your partner's.

D Now work in a group of four. Each pair can make up quiz questions about their own town and try them out on the other pair.

Speaking and writing

A Read the leaflet about London Walks on the page opposite and check any words you don't know in the dictionary.

B Finish the sentences in your own words.

1 London Walks is _____

_____.

2 They offer _____

_____.

3 The London Walks' guides include _____

_____

_____

_____

_____.

4 An archaeologist is someone who _____

_____.

5 The best thing about London Walks _____

_____

_____.

6 Your guide will be _____

_____.

7 To go on a walk, you don't _____

_____.

8 The walks take place _____

_____.

The original
LONDON WALKS

Summer 1999 *(March 26–November 2)*

We're **by far the oldest established** walking tour company in London and with nearly 35 years in the business we're confident we've got it right. In practice that means an astonishing variety of routes, utter reliability and – most important of all – **superb guides**.

The guides we represent are **the finest walking tour guides in London**. They include the author who is *"internationally recognised as the leading authority on Jack the Ripper"*; a distinguished BBC broadcaster and writer; the foremost authority on the Regent's Canal; an officer of the City of London Historical Society; a leading London archaeologist; the London tourist board's *Guide of the Year*; and several renowned actors and actresses.

It's a constellation of expertise, talent and experience that is without equal in this business and it's the key to our standing as London's *premier* walking firm.

To go on a walk, meet your guide and fellow walkers on the pavement just outside the designated Underground station at the time stated. Your guide will be holding up copies of this leaflet.

The **walks last about two hours** and end near Underground stations. There is no need to book. (NB large groups please phone and let us know you're coming.) **The walks take place rain or shine.**

C Put the conversation below in the correct order. Then look at the list of walks and role-play the conversation with your partner, swapping roles.

1 Hmm ... I'm not sure ... . Look, what about "In the footsteps of Sherlock Holmes"?
2 Well, what about "Spies' and Spycatchers' London" then?
3 Come on, then. Off we go!
4 I'm not sure if I want to know about ghosts. I'd prefer "Princess Diana's London".
5 Yes, that sounds great. OK, Sherlock Holmes it is.
6 No, I think this is going to be boring. Let's go on a more exciting walk.
7 I'd like to go on the "Ghosts of the Old City" walk. Would you like to come with me?

Old Westminster
Classic murders and crimes
The London of Oscar Wilde
The Beatles "In my life" walk
Ghosts of the Old City
Jack the Ripper's London
Shakespeare's London
Princess Diana's London
In the footsteps of Sherlock Holmes
Spies' and Spycatchers' London
The Old Soho pub walk

D You are entering a competition for a free weekend in a top London hotel.
In order to win, you have to complete this sentence in not more than 20 words:

I'd like to visit London because _____

_____.

Complete the slogan in a funny or clever way. Then vote for the best slogan in the class.

British regions

Before you listen ...

A Work with a partner. Match the two parts of words or phrases, then write the names in the correct box:

1	Stone	a	Towers
2	Holyrood	b	pottery
3	Edinburgh	c	henge
4	Alton	d	Pavilion
5	Ironbridge	e	mountain
6	Wedgwood	f	Gorge
7	Royal	g	Castle
8	Loch	h	house
9	Snowdon	i	Ness
10	Caernarfon	j	Festival

South of England

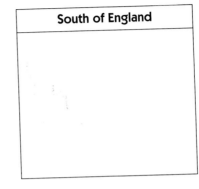

Scotland

Wales

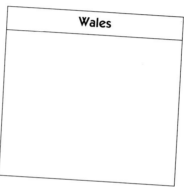

The Midlands and the North

B Write one sentence about each tourist attraction.

Example: *Stonehenge is an ancient stone circle on Salisbury Plain.*

Now listen

A Now listen and answer the questions:

1 Where is Madeleine from? _____

2 What is special about beaches in Devon and Cornwall? _____

_____

3 What will Madeleine find in St Ives? _____

4 How old are Saf's children? _____

5 Why is he worried about visiting stately homes? _____

_____

6 What could Saf and his wife see at Alton Towers? _____

7 What could the children do? _____

B Work with your partner. Role-play a conversation in a tourist office, asking and giving advice about visiting English regions.

Begin like this:
Student A: I would like to visit some interesting museums. Can you suggest anything?
Student B: Why, yes. You really should visit London. ...

Speaking and writing 💬 ✏️

A Read the leaflet about Hampton Court. Check any words you don't know in the dictionary and then answer the questions.

HAMPTON COURT PALACE

One of Henry VIII's most enduring passions was for his palace on the Thames.
To this day you can still experience the beauty that so enthralled him, as you stroll around six acres of magnificent buildings. Each and every corner will capture your heart.

THE KING'S APARTMENTS
Beneath the Colonnade in Clock Court is the entrance to the King's apartments, lovingly restored to their full glory after the fire of 1986. Here, you'll find the King's Great Bedchamber and his Eating Room as well as the magnificent King's Staircase.

RIVERSIDE GARDENS
Explore the 60 acres of beautiful gardens, then try unravelling our world famous maze.

HENRY VIII's STATE APARTMENTS
Up the staircase, beneath Anne Boleyn's Gateway, you'll find the state apartments of Henry VIII, the setting for some of the key events of his life. Here, he learnt of betrayal as well as experiencing the joy of seeing his son baptised. History will never have seemed so vivid.

1 Which king of England lived at Hampton Court?
2 In what year was there a fire?
3 What is the old-fashioned word for bedroom?
4 What is world famous in the gardens?
5 Which of Henry VIII's wives has a gateway named after her?
6 Do you think you would enjoy a visit to Hampton Court? Why (not)?

B Work with your partner. Play the part of a visitor to Hampton Court and your partner the tour guide. Write two questions to ask him/her. See if your partner can answer your questions, then swap roles.
Begin like this:
Excuse me, can you tell me which river is near the palace? …

C Choose one of the following activities.
   a Have you ever visited a stately home/important building? Write about your experience.
   b Write a visitor's guide for a historical monument/castle from your country.

English-English wordlist

pl = plural
sb = somebody
sth = something

A

abbey 76	a church with buildings attached where nuns or monks live
abbreviate 4	to shorten
ability 36 96 99	knowledge or skill to do sth
abroad 11	foreign countries
absolute rule 11	where one ruler has complete power
academic 39	relating to universities
accommodation 35 73	buildings where people live or stay
according to 28 68	as stated by sb/sth
accurate 66	precise
achieve 21	to succeed
acre 73	an area of land measuring 4047 square metres
activity holiday centre 87	a large area with different activities, especially sports, where people go on holiday
actually 51	really
AD (Anno Domini) 8	indicates that an event happened after the birth of Christ
advertise 20 66 77	to tell people about products on TV and in magazines etc.
advertisement 95	an announcement about a product
advice 110	words given or offered as an opinion
advise 8	to tell sb what you think they should do
affect 17 67	to influence
afford 7	to have enough money to buy sth
afternoon performance 47	a show at the theatre or a concert that occurs in the afternoon
age group 55	people who are all of a certain age
age: under age 57	not old enough to do sth
agree with 53 74	to have the same opinion as
aimed: be aimed at 55	to be directed at
air-raid shelter 66	where people go to protect themselves from attacks by aeroplanes
A level 36	an exam taken in Britain by 18-year-olds
allotment 33	a place to grow fruit and vegetables that is rented from the council
allow 11	to permit
ally 19	sb who is on your side
along 26 72	situated beside sth
along with 74	accompanied by
amazing 59	incredible
amount 7 73	quantity
amusement arcade 11	a place full of game machines
ancestor 14 17	a person from whom you are descended
angler 63	sb who fishes
announcer 102	a person who announces programmes on the radio
annoyed 51	angry
annual season ticket 70	a yearly entrance ticket, usually for football matches
appeal to 46	to find sth attractive
appear 102	to come into view
application 19	a formal request
apply for 99	to make a formal request for sth
apply to 38	to make a formal request to sb
applicant 99	sb who applies for sth
appoint 11 14	to choose sb for a job
appropriate 87	correct
archbishop 80	a bishop of the highest rank
area 4 20	region
arrange 27	to set out
arrange 53	to organise
assembly 37	a gathering of people
assent 16	agreement
assessment test 37	an exam to test sb's ability
attend to 29	to look after sb
attendances 60	the people present
attract 49	to provoke interest in sb/sth
authority 12 60	the power to give orders
average 57	standard
aviation industry 80	the building of planes
avoid 64 74	to keep oneself away from sb/sth
award 71 101	a prize
award 38	to give sb a prize
aware: make sb aware of 69	to show sth to sb

B

Bachelor of Arts 38   the degree given at university when you study languages, history, philosophy etc.

Bachelor of Education 38
the degree given at university when you study to become a teacher

Bachelor of Science 38
the degree given at university when you study science

background 10 52   conditions surrounding an event

ban 69   to stop sb from doing sth

bang on sth 29   to place your hand firmly on sth

bank cashier 42   a person who works in a bank dealing with the public

bank note 16   paper money

banker 41   the owner, director or manager of a bank

banking 21 42   the business of running a bank

bar chart 46   graph on which columns are used to show quantities

barge 73   a large flat-bottomed boat used on canals

bathe 80   to wash or swim

bathing pool 77   a swimming pool

battery hen 75   a hen kept in a small cage to produce eggs

BC 8   (Before Christ) indicates that an event happened before Christ was born

behead 64   to cut sb's head off

belong to 20 74   to be a member of

be made up 78   to consist of

bench 64   a long seat made of wood or stone

benefit from 52   to profit from

bike courier 40   sb who delivers parcels on a bike

bill 14   a draft of a new law

bin 74   a container for rubbish

bishop 14   a senior clergyman

blame 21   to say that sb is responsible for sth which has been badly done or is morally wrong

bless 28   to grant health, happiness and success

block of flats 32   a tall building consisting of lots of individual flats

blow up 27   to explode

board 94   daily meals in a hotel

boarding school 36   a school where pupils live during the term

boat racing competition 25
a contest where boats race one another

bonfire 27   a large fire made outdoors

border 8   the line dividing two countries

borrow 39   to receive sth temporarily from sb

bow 23   ribbon

bowl 61   a deep round dish

box: "the box" 56   the TV

branch 58   one of the shops that belongs to a chain-store

break down 33   to stop working

break (a record) 63   to beat a previous record

breed 22   to produce young

brilliant 89   excellent

bring alive 53   to give life to sth, to make sth interesting

bring together 48   to reconcile

broadcast 56 57   to show on television or transmit on radio

broadsheet 54   a serious newspaper

Brussels sprouts 27   vegetables like small cabbages

burn down 79   to destroy sth by fire

bypass 74   a road that goes round a town or city not through it

C

Cabinet 14   a group of the most important government ministers

call at 22   to visit

candlestick 28   a tall container that holds a candle

canoeing 87   travelling in a light boat using one or more paddles

caption 53   a short title under an illustration or article

care about 74   to be concerned for sb

care for 73   to look after sb

career 47   profession or occupation

carriage 16   part of a train, where people sit

carry on 16 86   to continue

carry out 35 78   to perform

casual 62   relaxed

catch 23   to stop and hold

cause 7 11 74   to make sth happen

cause 9   reason

cause: good cause 27
sth such as a charity that deserves public support

causeway 89   a raised road over low or wet ground

census 20   a survey

chain 78 87   a length of connected metal rings

chain-store 42 58   one of a series of shops owned by the same company

challenge 11   to ask sb to prove themselves

Chancellor of the Exchequer 14
the cabinet minister responsible for finance

Channel 56	the stretch of water between England and France
Channel Tunnel 30	the tunnel under the sea that links England and France
charity 23 58	a good cause
charity shop 58	a shop that sells second-hand items where the money goes to charity
chart 48	weekly list of best-selling pop music records
chart 55	a table
checked 84	examined
checkout operator 40	the person you pay at the supermarket
china 83	fine glazed white clay
chip 85	a small piece of silicon that carries a complex electrical circuit
chips 44	thin pieces of potato fried in fat
Christian 8 9 23	based on the teachings of Christ
Christianity 5 8 9	the religion based on the belief that Christ was the son of God
cinema box office 46	the place to buy tickets at the cinema
cinema complex 46	building where there is more than one cinema
circuit training 62	physical exercise based on a series of different exercises
claim 41	to demand or request
clan 84	a group of families, especially in Scotland, descended from a common ancestor
clean up 74	to make sth free of dirt
cloth 82 84	material
clubber 49	sb who goes to nightclubs regularly
coach 66	a vehicle pulled by horses
coast 27	land bordering the sea
coastal 72	near a coast
coastline 73	a length of coast
collapse 8	to fall down suddenly
collect 71	to gather together
college of further education 36	a place to study from the age of 16 where study does not lead to a degree
college of higher education 38	a place of study, generally after A levels, where study leads to a degree or other advanced qualification
coloniser 52	a person who settles in an area and takes control of it
column 76	a statue

combination 5	a mixture
combine 37	to mix
come back 26 29	to return
come in 56	to enter
commander 89	a person who gives orders
commodities 42	products that are exchanged in international trade
common 34	usual
community 29	the people living in one place
community centre 33	a place where people in the local area can meet
commute 66	to travel regularly to work from one's home
commuter 70	sb who travels to work
commuting 70	the act of travelling to work
company 19 20	a business
company 50	a theatre group
compete 46	to try to win by defeating others
competition 30 109	an event in which people compete
competitor 23	sb who enters a competition
complain 70	to say that you are unhappy about sth
complete 4	to finish
complete 29	to fill in
composer 47	sb who writes music
comprehensive school 36	a non fee-paying secondary school
compulsory 36	obligatory
concerned 74	worried
conductor 106	sb who sells tickets on a bus
confined space 31	a small, enclosed space
connect 108	to link together
conquer 87 88	to win
conqueror 9	sb who wins
conservation group 74	a group of people interested in protecting the environment
Conservative Party 15	a right-wing British political party
consist of 14 97	to be made up of
constituency 14	a district that has an elected representative in Parliament
contain 4 8 23 42	to hold
content 37	that which is contained in sth
controversial 51	likely to cause disagreement
convenience 67	the quality of being practical or suitable
convenience meal 45	a meal that is pre-cooked
convenient 57	easy
convert 8	to change religion
coronation 17	when a king or queen is crowned
cot 13	a bed for a baby

council housing 33   low-cost houses that are owned by the local authorities

council housing estate 33   a large area of houses that are owned by the local authorities

council tenant 33   sb who rents property from the local authorities

country cottage 33   a small house in the country

county 4   an administrative area in Britain

county council 4   the administrative body within a county

couple: a couple of 34   two

course 23   a place where horses race

course 38   a programme of study

court (of law) 12   a place where legal decisions are made

courtyard 39   an area within a building that has no roof

cover 55   the front of a magazine or book

cover 28   to place over sth

crash 29   to hit sth violently, making a loud noise

crisps 45   thin slices of potato, fried and dried

crossing 30   the act of going across the sea

crowd 29 86   a large group of people

crowded 77   filled with people

cup 24 60   an award

cure 43   sth that treats illnesses

custom 66   customers, people who buy things

custom 26   tradition, habit

D

daily 86   every day

damage 81   to spoil or break sth

date: out of date 17   old-fashioned, not relevant to the modern world

dawn 80   when the sun rises

deal with 46   to attend to

deep-fried 44   cooked in hot, deep fat

defeat 10 85   a conquest

defeat 9 10 88   to conquer

defender 10   sb who protects his position

degree 38   a qualification from university

delay 30   to cause sth to be late

deliver 54   to take sth to the place it is addressed to

demonstration 68 88   an organised protest

department 59   one of several divisions of a business or shop

Department of Transport 68   the part of the government that deals with transport

department store 59   a large shop with different departments

descent 87   the act of going down

despite 30   without being affected by sth

destroy 8 9 11 68   to ruin

detached house 32   a house that stands alone, having four outside walls

devote: devote time 60   to give one's time to sth

devoted 86   loyal

devoted: devoted to sport 56   which shows only sport

director 46   the person in charge

disabled 67   having a physical problem that makes it difficult to carry out certain everyday actions

disease 43   an illness

disk drive 85   the part of a computer where the floppy disk is inserted

display 26 59   show

display: on display 78   on show

display 26   to show

double dealing 53   cheating, not being honest

double-decker bus 67   a bus with two levels

draw 66   to pull

dreadful 74   awful

dress up 25   to wear smart clothes

drift 73   to be carried along by air or water

driving licence 4   the document that legally permits sb to drive a car

drop out 39   to leave school or university before completing one's study

drum 29   a cylindrical musical instrument played by hitting it with sticks or one's hands

dry-stone walling 73   the building of a stone wall without using cement

dub 53   to replace the original language of a film with a different language

dubbed 56   having all the dialogue in a different language to the original

due: due to open 30   the time sth should open

dumpling 44   a small ball of dough that is steamed or boiled

Dutch 31   sb/sth from Holland

E

edge 74   the outside limit

elaborate 8   complicated and highly decorated

elderly 34 69   old

enter 71   to go into

entertain 16 — to receive sb as a guest
entertaining 51 — enjoyable
environmental 74 — relating to the environment
erect 76 — to build sth
estate 33 — an area of houses
event 24 93 — sth that happens
exhaust fumes 67 — gases that come from a car
exhibition 26 78 — a display
expand 42 76 77 — to grow bigger
expense: at the expense of 15 — at the cost of
experience 50 — to gain knowledge from certain events
experiment 78 — a trial
extend 66 — to make sth longer

facility 105 — equipment
fail 39 — to be unsuccessful
fairly 99 — quite
fall apart 52 — to break
fancy 22 — to find sb attractive
fare 71 — money paid to do something
fashionable 43 51 81 — in fashion
fast 23 — a period of not eating
feature 95 — sth that is characteristic
fierce 38 — angry or aggressive
fill in 46 — to complete sth
filling 44 — a mixture to put in cakes, pies etc.
fill shelves 40 — to put lots of objects onto shelves
fine 69 — to punish by being ordered to pay a sum of money
flee 9 — to escape
fleet 10 — a collection of ships
flood 13 — to arrive in very large numbers
flyer 49 — a leaflet
foreign currency 42 — money from other countries
foreign exchange 42 — a place where you buy and sell foreign currency
forestry 85 — the practice of planting and caring for trees
former 5 13 52 — the one before
found 42 — to start
founder 28 — sb who creates an organisation or business
fringe theatre 47 — unconventional theatre productions
front bench 15 — the place where the leading members of the government and opposition sit in Parliament
fuel 19 — material burned to produce heat or power

fund 19 — to save a sum of money for a particular purpose
funky 53 — fashionable
futures market 42 — the market of buying and selling goods

G

gain 88 — to increase by
gambling 17 — playing games for money
gateway 111 — entrance
GCSE 36 — General Certificate of Secondary Education
Georgian 80 — of the time of the British kings George I – IV (1714-1830)
get around to 66 — to finally do sth after attending to other matters
get together 57 — to meet up
glen 85 — a narrow valley, especially in Scotland
go back to 8 — to date back to
go down 42 — to decrease
good value 44 — when the price is right
goods 73 — items that are bought and sold
grade 38 — mark, level of exam result
graduate 38 — sb who left university with a degree
grammar school 36 — a type of secondary school
grant 39 — money given for a particular purpose
guess 22 41 — to give an answer without being sure if it is correct
Gujerati 13 — the language of the Gujarat in West India, or a native of the Gujarat
Gulf War 19 — the war that occurred in 1991 when Iraq invaded Kuwait

H

hand: on the other hand 75 — by contrast
handle 27 — to deal with sth
hands-on 78 — practically involved
hardcore 48 — basic
head of state 16 — chief public representative of a country
head: the head of a household 34 — the person responsible for a family
headline 54 — words printed in large type on the front page of a newspaper
headteacher 54 — the head of a school
heat up 45 — to warm up
heavy: heavy traffic 74 — when there is a lot of traffic
hedge 73 — a row of bushes planted closely together

heir 10 87	the person who will receive property when the owner dies
hereditary peer 14	a title passed on from one generation to another
high-rise 33	very tall blocks of flats
high-street shop 59	a shop situated on the main street of a town
higher education 38	education at university
highlight 60	the most interesting part
hiking 87	long walks in the country
holiday resort 26 81	a place where people go on holiday
holiday-maker 73	a tourist
homeland 86	where sb originally comes from
homeless 35	without a home
host 82	a person who receives and entertains guests
hostel 35	a cheap place to stay
Houses of Parliament 14	the House of Commons and House of Lords
household 34 57	the members of a family
housing 4	places to live
hurdles 63	a series of upright frames to be jumped over

illuminated 8	lit up
impressive 87	which makes a strong impression
improve 22	to make sth better
in-house 39	done by a company itself, not by freelancers
include 4 27 43 53 97	to make sb/sth part of a larger group
income support 41	money given to people who do not earn much or who are unemployed
inconvenient 30	not practical, difficult
indie 48	independent (type of music)
industrialist 83	sb who works in industry
informal 12 62	relaxed
ingredient 44	the food you need to make a recipe
injure 67 88	to hurt
instead 20 36 85	as an alternative
instructor 62	sb who teaches sth
introduce 37 66	to bring in
introduce 56	to present sth
invade 8 9 10	to enter a country by force
invader 8 9	sb who enters a country by force
invest 43 68	to put money into
invite sb round 32	to ask sb to your house
involved in 17 43	concerned with
isolated 69 81	alone
issue 54	topic

J

join 19	to become a member
join 88	to become part of
join in 29	to take part in
joint 61	shared
joke: play a joke on 23	to do sth to sb in order to cause amusement
judiciary 16	judges of a collective country
jump the queue 6	to go to the front of the queue
jumbled up 101 104	mixed up

K

kebab house 45	a place where you can buy kebabs
keen 19	enthusiastic
keep out 30	to stop sb from entering
kick 61	to hit sth with the foot
kids 77	children, young people
knock 26	a sharp blow

L

lamp-post 64	a tall post supporting a street lamp
landowner 73	sb who owns a lot of land
lands 88	areas
landscape 87	scenery
last 17	to endure
law 7 38	the rules governing a country
law 14	an individual set of rules concerning a specific area of activity
Law Courts 77	the room or buildings in which cases are heard
lawn 33 39	an area of grass in a garden
lead 5	a strap for controlling a dog
lead 62	to guide
leaflet 71 83	a printed sheet of paper
leafy 72	covered in leaves
lecture 38 77	a talk
lecturer 38	sb who gives a talk
left-wing 15	supporting socialism
legal system 84	a system of law
Lent 23	the period of 40 days and nights from Ash Wednesday to the day before Easter, observed as a time of penitence
level 37 62	a point on a scale
library 4 13	a collection of books for reading or borrowing
lie 16	to rest
life peer 14	sb who is made a peer for life
lift up 29	to raise
lighthouse 73	a tower containing a light to warn or guide ships
likely 13 67	probably

line 66 — where trains run on

link 18 31 — a connection

link: be linked to 12 29 — to be connected to

live 48 — transmitted as it is happening, not recorded

living: earn a living 72 — to earn enough money for one's needs

loads of 62 — many

local education authority 39 — the body who is responsible for education in a certain area

loch 85 — a Scottish word for "lake"

look after 4 12 40 74 — to be responsible for sb

look for 66 75 78 — to search

look like 64 — to resemble

look round 56 85 — to turn one's head to see something

loss 7 — the act of losing sth

lost 6 — which cannot be found

loudspeaker 43 — the part of a stereo system etc. from which the sound comes

low impact workout 62 — exercises that are not strenuous

M

main 15 53 — most important

main line route 70 — a train route between major places

mainly 9 12 — for the most part

maintain 98 — to keep

make sure 6 9 — to be certain

make-up 55 — powder, lipstick etc. put on the face to make it more attractive

manage 77 — to achieve sth

manufacture 11 43 82 — to make, to construct

manufacturer 58 — sb who makes things

march 9 — to walk as soldiers do

marching 24 — the act of walking as soldiers do

mark 28 — a stain

maroon 36 — a brownish red

match 28 — to link one thing with another

mate 62 — a friend

materials 43 — substances

maypole 24 — a decorated pole that people dance around on May 1st

maze 79 — a network of hedges designed as a puzzle through which one must find a way

mean 13 14 — to intend

meaning 12 — significance

medicine 43 — a substance used in curing illnesses or disease

meet 14 — to come together

mellow 48 — soft

Member of Parliament 14 — an elected representative in the House of Commons

member state 16 — a country that belongs to a certain organisation

mention 6 45 53 — to refer to

meter 66 — sth that counts how much money to pay

minimum wage 40 — the lowest wage that an employer can pay sb by law

minority group 56 — a small group of people

mistress 10 — a woman who is having an affair with a married man

mixed up 26 — confused

moor 51 81 — an open area of high land

moped 69 — a motor cycle with pedals and a small engine

motivator 62 — sb or sth that gives encouragement

MP 14 — Member of Parliament

multiracial 21 — made up of different races

multicoloured 27 — made up of different colours

mutton 12 — meat from a fully grown sheep

mystery 47 — sth that is impossible to explain

myth 89 — a legend

N

national anthem 86 — song or hymn adopted by a country and sung to express patriotism

national curriculum 37 — the document that says what subjects should be studied at school

native 9 13 — being a local inhabitant

nature reserve 73 — a protected area of countryside often having rare plants or animals

nearby 82 — close to

neither 18 — not one nor the other

network 67 — a closely linked group of people

no longer 11 73 — not anymore

notice 12 — to become aware of sth

novel 50 — a story in the form of a book

novelist 21 50 — sb who writes novels

nowadays 13 23 30 — at the moment

nursery 40 — a place where children are cared for while their parents are at work

nursery school 36 — a school for children aged 2-5

O

observatory 79 — a building from which the stars can be observed

obsessed 75 — thinking about sb/sth continuously

off: off the coast 84 — in the sea but relatively close to land

offering 29 — a donation

oil refining 43 — the act of removing impurities from oil

old-fashioned 71 — out of date

open countryside 77 — country away from towns or suburbs

opposite 15 — as different as possible to sth

order 26 — sequence

organically grown 45 — grown without the use of synthetic chemicals

original 12 19 30 76 — first, earliest

orphan 50 — sb without any parents

otherwise 23 26 45 — if not

overflow 74 — to flow over the edges or limits

overrun 8 — attacked

overseas 11 — in a foreign country

own 11 32 — to possess

own 4 12 — belonging to oneself

own: on one's own 34 69 — alone

owner 83 — the person who owns sth

P

pagan 8 24 26 — being sb who does not believe in Christianity

palm 79 81 — a plant or tree that grows in hot countries

pantomime 27 92 — a type of play with music and dancing which is popular especially around Christmas

paperboy/girl 54 — sb who delivers newspapers to people's houses

park 59 — a public open space with gardens, trees and lakes etc.

part 4 9 — component

partner 7 27 — one of two people

pass 16 — to move forward

past 73 — time gone by

pattern 29 — an arrangement of shapes, lines and colours

pay back 39 — to return money

pay for 18 36 — to give money for sth

pedestrian 67 — sb who walks on the pavement

penalty 68 — a punishment for breaking the law

people: different peoples 8 — different races or tribes

people 9 — persons

per cent 13 — number in a hundred

perform 25 47 — to sing, dance, act or play music

performance 47 53 — an event where people sing, dance, act

performer 86 — sb who performs

Persian 13 — the language that is spoken in Persia

pet 59 — an animal kept in the home such as a dog or cat

petrol 43 — the fuel that gives cars power

pick up 53 61 — to take hold of sth

pick up 66 — to meet sb casually

pilgrim 80 — sb who visits a place of religious significance

pillar box 64 — a postbox in the street where you post letters

pit 82 — a mine

place 38 — an area or position

plain 80 — dull

plan 6 75 — an idea

plan 27 — to make arrangements

plan 78 — a map

platform 71 — flat surface at a railway station where you board and leave trains

play 25 29 49 — a drama

playwright 50 — sb who writes plays

pleased 33 — happy

pleasure boat 73 — a boat used for enjoyment only, not for commercial purposes

plot 27 — the outline of a story

policy 14 — a statement of ideas and aims

pollutants 67 — things that dirty the atmosphere

pony-trekking 87 — travelling on a pony for pleasure

poor house 50 — a place in Victorian times where poor people lived

populated: densely populated 72 — where many people live close together

posh 44 — luxurious

pot noodle 45 — a meal of noodles in a pot to which you add boiling water

power 9 10 11 — might

power 75 — energy

practise 28 — to do sth repeatedly to improve one's skills

pram 67 — a four-wheeled carriage pushed by hand for a baby

pregnant 10 — the state of carrying a baby before giving birth

previous 99 — earlier, former

principality 87 — a country ruled by a prince

print out 78 — to produce sth in a printed form

prize 22 52 — award

produce 4 11 60 73 — to create

production 47 — a performance

properly 7 — suitably, adequately

protect 67 73	to keep sb/sth safe from harm
prove 62	to show that sth is true
pub sign 64	a sign hanging outside a pub
public company 70	a company that sells shares to the public
public life 21	life in the public eye, for example of people in government
public school 60	a school where parents pay fees
publish 17 51	to prepare and print a book
pull down 33	to destroy
pull up 73	to remove
pumpkin 26	a large round fruit with many seeds
Punjab 48	an area in India
puppet 53	a doll or small figure that is controlled by strings or one's hands
push forward 6	to use force to move sth forwards
put back 65	to return sth to its place
put on 27	to perform or organise a show
put together 13	associated, linked

Q

queue 6 25	a line of people waiting for sb/sth
quite 32	reasonably
quiz 41	a competition in which people try to answer questions to test their knowledge

R

race 23	a competition
racial prejudice 56	dislike of people of different races
ragga 48	a type of music
raise 19 23	to collect
raise 73	to bring up
range 46	variety
range 44	to vary
rant 53	to speak loudly and incoherently
rap 48	a type of music
rapping 53	speaking using the rhythms of rap
rating 57	classification or ranking
rave 48	a type of music
raw cotton 82	unrefined cotton
raw materials 11	materials that have not been treated
reach 87	to extend to
reaction 53 88	response
read aloud 53	to read out loud
ready: get ready 57	to prepare
rebel 9 52	to resist authority
recognise 18 76 86	to be able to identify sb/sth
recommend 100	to praise sth as suitable
record 51	account
record 48	a vinyl disc that contains audible music

record 57	to keep an account of sth
recover 27	to get better
reduce 21 43 67 86	to make sth smaller
refugee 20	a person who has been forced to leave his country and live in another country
registration 37	the act of registering
registry office 35	where people get married in a civil ceremony
rejoin 18	to put back together
relations 22	relatives
relationship 19	the state of being connected to sb
release 39	to set free
relevant 29	connected to
rely on 18	to depend on
remain 86	to stay
remote 69	far away
rent 32 57	to pay for the occupation or use of sth
rent 39	weekly or monthly payment for the use of sth
replace 33	to put sth back in place
report 54	to give an account of sth
reputation 6 39 58 86	the way people think of sb
requirement 99	what is necessary
research chemist 42	a chemist who does research
restore 10	to return
retailing 42	the selling of goods
revival 13 86	bringing back to health
rid: get rid of 5	to free oneself of sth
ride 83	form of entertainment at a fair or theme park
right 8	true, correct
right to vote 11	the possibility to vote
right-wing 15	conservative
rise 10 11	emergence
rise 21 41 62	to increase
risk: to be at risk from sth 69	to be in danger of sth
roll 23	a small loaf of bread
Romance languages 12	languages descended from Latin
round trip 87	a trip where you return to your point of departure
rowing 25	using a boat with oars
rubbish disposal 4	getting rid of waste
rude 6	not polite
rugged 88	rough
rule 9	authority
rule 60	a regulation
run 4	to administer, to organise
run 25	to flow
run 30 70	to operate

run 56	to be shown	
rush hour 6 68	the busiest time of the day to travel when people are going to and from work	

S

safe 33	secure
safety 67	security
sailing 87	travelling by boat or ship
sailing ship 79	a ship that moves forward using sails
sales assistant 42	sb who works in a shop
salmon 44 63	a large fish with pink flesh
savoury 44	tasty and not sweet
saying 77	a commonly said phrase
scary 26	frightening
scenery 72	landscape
scholarship 18	an award of money to a student
school leaver 39	sb who has left school
scientific paper 13	an article on a scientific subject
Scottish 4 5 8	sb/sth from Scotland
screen test 78	an audition for a film
seat 14	being elected to Parliament
second-hand 58	sth that has been used before
secondary school 36	school for pupils aged 11-18 in England
see in 22	to welcome
self-sufficient 73	able to exist alone
self-government 87	the right of the people of a region to choose their own government
semi-circle 15	half a circle
semi-detached house 32	a house that is attached on one side to another
semi-skilled 20	having some training, but less than a skilled worker
serials: as serials 50	in individual sections
set: to be set in (of film, book) 50	to happen at a particular time
set an example 17	to show sb how to behave through your own behaviour
set off 27	to begin
set up 80	to erect
set up 8 19 50	to start
settle 8 9	to make a home
shadow cabinet 14	the cabinet in opposition to the government
shipyard 85	a place where ships are built
shopping complex 59	a place where there are many different shops
shorthand 99	a method of writing quickly using symbols
sick of 53	fed up with

sightseeing bus 77	a bus specially for tourists
sign 64	a symbol
sign on 41	to register
sing along 25	to accompany a song
single 48	a record with only one song on either side
single 41	without a partner or husband/wife
single parent 41	a parent without a partner or husband/wife
single-sex 36	only male or only female
slope 87	incline
snooker 61	a game played with 15 red balls and 7 other coloured balls on a billiard table
soap 56	substance used for washing and cleaning
so-called 20	known as
socialise 80	to spend time with other people
socialising 39	being with other people
sociologist 53	sb who studies people's behaviour
solve 21	to find an answer to sth
soul 26	the spiritual part of a person
sound 17 51	to seem
spa town 80	a town where there is a spring of mineral water with healing properties
spa water 80	water that comes from a spa
spare time 73	time not spent working
spell 53	a magical charm
spicy 44	having a strong, hot flavour due to the use of seasonings
split 70	broken in two
split up 4	divided
spoil 75	to ruin
spread 8 9 13	to extend
spring 80	a place where water comes to the surface
squirt 26	to force out in a thin stream
staff 39 59	the people that work in a company
stage: on stage 48	performing
stand for 65	to mean sth
stand-by 47	an unreserved ticket
standard 37 73	usual
state banquet 16	a large formal meal hosted by a country
state channel 56	a TV channel owned and run by government institutions
state school 36	a non fee-paying school
stately home 83	a grand house of historical interest
state-run 96	run by government institutions
stay in 35	to remain inside
stay on 37	to continue to remain
steamed 44	cooked by the steam from boiling water
steel 85	a strong metal

steel band 25	a West Indian band who use empty oil drums as instruments
steel industry 82	the industry that makes steel
steps 67	stairs
stop 8	to put an end to sth
stop 68	to forbid sth
storey 33	a level in a building
storyline 56	a plot
stretch 30	a piece of water
stretch 87	to extend
stuck: get stuck 67	to not be able to move
subscribe to 56	to contribute to
suggest 110	to put forward an idea
suitable 31	appropriate
sun worship 80	considering the sun as sacred
superstore 59	a huge shop
support 19	to give help and encouragement to sb
surrender 8 87	to give in
surround 76	to move into position all around sb/sth
surrounding 59	which are all around sb/sth
survey 35	an examination
swap 111	to exchange
sweet 23	sugary

T

table 29	a diagram
tabloid 54	a newspaper that prints less serious stories
take back 5 58	to return sth
take off 31	to leave the ground and begin to fly
take on 40	to undertake
take out 79	to remove
take part in 22 62	to participate in sth
take place 24	to happen
talks 88	discussions
tapestry 12	a woven pattern or picture
tartan 84	a pattern of coloured stripes, traditionally from Scotland
tattoo 85	a military show
taxi fare 31	the amount you pay for a taxi ride
tea clipper 79	a ship that carries tea
team 60	a group of sports people
temp 40	sb who works temporarily, usually a secretary
tend to 12 44	to be likely to behave in a certain way
term 4	an expression
term 38	a period of time
terraced house 32	one of a row of houses which are all attached to each other
test 36 66	an exam

test 58	to give sb an exam
test match 61	a cricket match between teams of certain countries
theme park 83	a park with entertainment rides
think of oneself as 4	to consider oneself to be sth
throne 16	the seat a king or queen sits on
throughout 13 20 24 43	during the whole of
throw back 63	to return sth by throwing it
throw out 50	to get rid of
time-consuming 30	which takes a long time
tip 72 81	end
tomb 50	the place where sb is buried
top 88	highest part or point
top-quality 43	high quality
tour guide 111	a guide who takes tourists to visit sites
tournament 60	competition
tower block 33	a tall block of flats
town planning 4	the organisation of roads, buildings, parks etc. for a town
track 70	the lines that trains run on
trade 13 19	buying and selling
trade in 9	to buy and sell sth
trader 9	sb who buys and sells
traffic fumes 7	the gases that come from cars
traffic-jam 73	a line of non-moving traffic
trailer 46	a low vehicle, often like a box with wheels, which is pulled by another vehicle
train spotting 71	the act of identifying different trains from their numbers
training scheme 39	a programme of learning and work experience
treat 26	sth that gives great pleasure
trendy 49	fashionable
trick: play a trick on sb 26	to deceive sb
trick or treat 26	an American tradition that occurs on Halloween when children visit houses asking for treats, or they play tricks
tube station 66	station on the London Underground
tune 25	song
turn into 25	to become
tutorial 38	a lesson at university
TV listings magazine 55	a magazine that contains all the times of TV programmes
tycoon 13	a very rich person

U

undergraduate 38	sb studying for a degree at university